# MOMISTRY

"Being a Mom is Ministry"

PATTY NOEL

Copyright © 2022 Patty Noel

All rights reserved. No part of this book may be reproduced or used in any manner without the prior written permission of the copyright owner, except for the use of brief quotations in a book review.

ISBN: 9798424231223

Beta-reading by Marsha Garrett, Esther Scoggin, and Rachel Newhouse
Editing by Hannah Noel, Tracy O'Brien, and Rachel Newhouse
Layout by Rachel Newhouse for elfinpen designs
Cover by Treasure Advertising

DISCLAIMER: Some names have been changed to protect individuals' privacy. This book does not replace the advice of a medical or mental health professional. Consult your physician before making any changes to your diet or regular health plan. These are my memories, from my perspective, and I have tried to represent events as faithfully as possible.

Unless otherwise indicated, all Scripture quotations are taken from the Holy Bible, New Living Translation, copyright © 1996, 2004, 2015 by Tyndale House Foundation. Used by permission of Tyndale House Publishers, Carol Stream, Illinois 60188. All rights reserved.

Scripture quotations marked TPT are taken from The Passion Translation®. Copyright © 2017, 2018, 2020 by Passion & Fire Ministries, Inc. Used by permission. All rights reserved. ThePassionTranslation.com.

Scripture quotations marked NIV are taken from the Holy Bible, New International Version®, NIV®. Copyright © 1973, 1978, 1984, 2011 by Biblica, Inc.™ Used by permission of Zondervan. All rights reserved worldwide. www.zondervan.com The "NIV" and "New International Version" are trademarks registered in the United States Patent and Trademark Office by Biblica, Inc.™

Scripture quotations marked NKJV are taken from the New King James Version®. Copyright © 1982 by Thomas Nelson. Used by permission. All rights reserved.

Scripture quotations marked GNT are taken from the Good News Translation in Today's English Version- Second Edition Copyright © 1992 by American Bible Society. Used by Permission.

Scripture quotations marked AMP are taken from the Amplified® Bible (AMP), Copyright © 2015 by The Lockman Foundation. Used by permission. www.lockman.org

Scripture quotations marked (NLT) are taken from the Holy Bible, New Living Translation, copyright ©1996, 2004, 2015 by Tyndale House Foundation. Used by permission of Tyndale House Publishers, Carol Stream, Illinois 60188. All rights reserved.

# CONTENTS

| | |
|---|---|
| Acknowledgements | I |
| Introduction | V |
| Chapter 1: What is Momistry? | 1 |
| Chapter 2: Be FREE to be a Momma Bear | 19 |
| Chapter 3: Find a Mentor and Fill Your Toolbelt | 47 |
| Chapter 4: Parenting in a Sexualized Culture | 67 |
| Chapter 5: Being Married (or a Single Mom) with Children | 109 |
| Chapter 6: "I Will Never Be Like My Mother." | 129 |
| Chapter 7: How Do People Afford Children? | 149 |
| Chapter 8: What Do Healthy Boundaries Look Like? | 167 |
| Chapter 9: Oh, So Many Opinions with So Many Choices | 183 |
| Chapter 10: HELP | 203 |
| Chapter 11: Then They're Grown | 217 |
| Chapter 12: Welcome to Your Momistry | 229 |
| Resources | 239 |

# ACKNOWLEDGEMENTS

**Give thanks to the Lord, for He is good! His faithful love endures forever.**

**Psalm 107:1**

Jesus, oh, thank You, Jesus. I'd regret not giving Him my first acknowledgement. He saved and rescued me to live an abundant life now. He has *only* been good to me and my family. He has lavished His love on me and my family, unto a thousand generations. Thanks a quadrillion, Jesus.

Stuart Noel: My husband, my sexy soldier-man, and my biggest fan. He encourages and sometimes even pushes me to be all that God has called me to be. Through the nights of me ugly crying and moments of doubt and all the feelings of total inadequacy, he lovingly held me. He brushed the tears away and reminded me of who God says I am. There were so many times that I heard Stuart say, "Patty, if God told you to do it, just do it. It's not about you." Yep, he's a rock-solid man of faith, an oak tree of righteousness, and I'm so thankful to be planted next to him. Thanks a quadrillion, Jesus.

Our children in order of age:

Ian, our eldest son, for forgiving me and still loving me after *all* of my mom fails. Even after so much heartache, he has never changed his mind about God. His Dad (Stuart) and I could not be more proud of the man, husband, and father he's become. Thanks a quadrillion, Jesus.

Jessica, our eldest daughter, for her love for Jesus and for family. And now for being one of my very best friends. Jesus is still, and will always be, her first love. She is always such an encouragement to me. As she now walks in her own Momistry, is a wonderful wife, and is an extremely successful entrepreneur. We couldn't be more proud of her. Thanks a quadrillion, Jesus.

Andrew, our middle son, whom I didn't birth, but has always treated me with great honor as his mom. As he was growing up, Andrew's passion for God was inspiring. Now, he loves God in a more cognitive way while holding onto the powerful God experiences from his youth. He is an uber-smart, successful businessman and influencer. His dad and I are so very proud of him. Thanks a quadrillion, Jesus.

Samuel, our youngest son, who cheers loudly and constantly for me (and everyone) to do the things that God has created them to do. His zeal for God and love for people is contagious. His dad and I are amazed as we watch Samuel as a youth leader, adoring husband, faithful dog dad, and flourishing entrepreneur who is changing the world with the love of Jesus. We are very proud. Thanks a quadrillion, Jesus.

Natalie, our youngest daughter, whom I also didn't birth. We are so grateful that God brought her to us to be her family and to me to be her mom. When we adopted her, she changed her middle name to Joy, as God has restored her joy. Her dad and I are so excited to watch her walk out her destiny with God. Thanks a quadrillion, Jesus.

All five of our children love God, honor their parents, and love their families fiercely. They are my legacy. My life serving them in the Momistry has been well spent. Thanks a quadrillion, Jesus.

Pastor Tom and Pastor Diana Trout: This couple prayed for me and my family when I didn't have any strength to pray. They stood by us through many storms and seasons of life. They spoke hard truths to Stuart and I out of a love that empowered us to change our lives. Their living example of faith and family has always been exemplary. They are our pastors, our mentors, and our dear, forever friends. Thanks a quadrillion, Jesus.

**But I lavish unfailing love for a thousand generations on those who love me and obey my commands.**

**Exodus 20:6**

# INTRODUCTION

> **Your most important disciples are sitting at your kitchen table.**
> **Toby Mac, Speak Life**

The purpose of this book is to help younger mothers and mothers-to-be avoid some of the mistakes and pitfalls that my husband and I fell into. After parenting for well over 30 years, we have made many. *"Likewise with the female elders, lead them into lives free from gossip and drunkenness and to be teachers of beautiful things. This will enable them to teach the younger women to love their husbands, to love their children, and to be self-controlled and pure, taking care of their household and being devoted to their husbands. By doing these things the word of God will not be discredited." (Titus 2:3-5 TPT).* As you read these verses in Titus, it says "to teach the younger women to love their husbands [which is not always an easy task] and to love their children [also, not always an easy task]."

For me, life was hard at times. I sure needed someone to help me stay the course. Someone that was an older, experienced mom and wife. Get ready as we go on this journey through chapters full of powerful life lessons. I like to call these lessons "life nuggets" or "tools for your toolbelt"; they are practical applications packed with numerous personal stories. Each chapter ends with thought-provoking questions to journal about, as well as ample space for note taking. Feel free to mark this book up, highlight, dog ear pages, circle, underline, and pray, pray, pray.

I'm not a perfect parent or wife; there is no such thing. If you think there is such a person, it's a mirage. There are countless illusions to perfection you will see all over social media. Those are carefully filtered and fabricated snippets of a movie, and you don't ever see the whole reel. Have you ever watched a movie based on a great trailer, only to walk away shockingly disappointed? Yeah, that's kind of what social media represents. The comparison on these sites can be overwhelmingly exasperating. Be encouraged as you digest the chapters in this book to parent God's way and laugh at some "real life, behind-the-scenes stories of my parenting journey."

This generation of moms has a massive amount of news feeds, threads, and videos trying to ensnare them with the trap of comparison. With that being said, next time you see one of those posts or videos, just bless that momma on her good day, and remember the hundreds of good days you've been blessed with—even if today you're washing your third load of puke-covered laundry, and you're staring at the steamer you rented in an attempt to remove the vomit stains and smell off the carpets (and let's not even mention out of the car). Your coffee was ice cold an hour ago, your messy bun is more than a mess, and you haven't showered for five days. This will pass. Be encouraged that the good days by far outweigh the bad, but there will be some that are bad and hard and sad and difficult. There will be days when you feel like you just want to run or disappear. If you've ever read my blogs on our website or on our Facebook group Her Entourage, or heard me speak publicly, you've most certainly heard me say "Momming is the best job ever and the hardest job ever. YOU CAN DO IT!"

On Facebook I'm the co-founder of a large Christian women's private group called Her Entourage. Before writing this book, we did a survey of the moms, foster moms, stepmoms, guardians, and moms-to-be in the group. We asked 10 questions regarding what their biggest concerns were with mothering. It was an anonymous survey, so the response was huge. Several women shared it around and we were able to pool statistics from a diverse group of hundreds of mommas. The purpose was to gather information to address relevant issues in blogs and in this book. You will hear me refer to Her Entourage and the survey throughout the book.

My husband and I were married twenty-six years ago. We are a blended family. I entered our marriage with two children and he with one. We lost a baby at twenty weeks of pregnancy within the first year of our marriage. The second year, God gave us a bouncing baby boy. Twenty-two years later, when we were empty-nesters in our early fifties, God brought us a ten-year-old girl, whom we adopted when she was eleven. We have four sons (one in heaven) and two daughters. I've had jobs and careers, but momming has been my favorite by far.

As I'm writing this, we have four grandchildren and three amazing sons- and daughters-in-law. In this book I will refer to them as in-loves, not in-laws. Lisa Bevere used this phrase in her books, and it stuck with me. We are under a covenant of love, not law.

In addition to our children and grandchildren, our home has hosted well over thirty people—many Bible school students, some pastors, a few foster children, extended family members, and children of close friends. Nearly all of the young people who have lived with us chose to refer to me as Patty Mom, which after several years has sort of stuck. We have been serving at the same church for over twenty years and have done all sorts of different ministries. I've finally settled into mine in Momistry.

As for quality parenting, it took years of trial and error, with the first fifteen years being mostly error. Thankfully, children are quite forgiving. When I was a young mom, other than people making snarky comments, I didn't have the much-needed positive, consistent influence from successful parents or mentors that I was starving for. Because of this, I spent years flopping around like a fish out of water in this whole mothering gig. God did, mercifully, bring to me some amazing pastors/friends and also some life-changing books, seminars, tape series (cassette tapes to be exact), and so on. Human nature is to do what we know, and all I knew to do was what I had seen my mom, dad, and their families do. They had all been raised in dysfunctional and borderline abusive homes.

My mom could be the sweetest person you've ever met in your life, but she could also become angry, name-call, face slap, give the silent treatment, and slam things, which was not the example I wanted to follow with my children. Over years and years, mothering became more natural as I used some of the tools I'd been given. Listen, if I can change and break unhealthy family patterns or traditions, so can you. With the Holy Spirit, we *all* can. *"I can do all this through him who gives me strength." (Philippians 4:13 NIV)*

Since I'm an approachable person, and openly and sometimes quite directly share experiences with other moms, I receive a lot of urgent calls. Over twenty years ago, a mom called me late one night. She had found sexually explicit photos on her eleven-year-old's phone. We talked through many things (one being, why does an 11-year-old need a phone?) and prayed. Since that call, I have received dozens and dozens of other calls, texts, and emails and have gone on endless amounts of coffee dates to discuss similar topics related to electronics. We are living in a dangerously digital age.

One time I shared a hodgepodge story in a blog I wrote on Her Entourage regarding the topic of kids and electronics. The post received a surprising amount of traction with a lot of dialogue, comments, and sharing. Since I had spoken with so many mommas over the years, the blog I posted had become a mixture of stories without any specific faces or names associated with it. Parenting kids with electronics is such a prevalent issue in society today, thus we must have the tools to try to fix the problems associated with it—instead of boxing in the air or getting angry and yelling or crying and making your child feel ashamed. As soon as you realize that thousands, if not **Parenting without wise counsel, active grandparents, or role models was never in God's plan for humanity**. hundreds of thousands, of other moms are having to work through the same things, it becomes a bit easier and a *lot* less personal. We will talk more about this later in the book as I share some of my experiences with you.

As a mom of thirty-four years, I have learned a lot, gained several tools, helped other mommas, and am now having so much fun as a grandma bear. If I can share some, or even most, of the tools I've learned along the way and help other mommas not blunder away their first fifteen years of parenting, that would be awesome. Parenting without wise counsel, active grandparents, or role models was never in God's plan for humanity. His plan was always for the elder men and women to train the younger (see Titus 2:3-5). In America, we have a pretty dysfunctional culture of independence, isolation, and, dare I say, even rebellion. God is big on families and community, and it's in our best interest to get back to doing things His way.

As I mentioned, at the end of each chapter you will find: a prayer, some questions or challenges, and an area for notes. Those portions are meant for you to do some self-reflection. This will be where you can write down what God is saying to you while you're reading. Please make sure to pray out loud. You want to hear with your ears the powerful declarations and life changing words. As I write, publish, and distribute this book, my hope is that it becomes a tool in your toolbelt, a tool to help you build a family that loves, serves, and honors God from generation to generation. My prayer is that you will walk away from reading this book knowing that you're not alone and that you have an entourage of women cheering you on. I also want you to feel empowered and equipped to fulfill your calling in Momistry.

**So much love,
@pattymom_**

# CHAPTER 1

## What is Momistry?

```
MOM*ISTRY

/ma~mastre~/

The   work   or   vocation   of
dedicating  your  life  to  the
ministry of raising children
who love God and love family.
Keeping children in your care
safe: body, soul, and spirit.
```

For my dad's eightieth birthday, I joined him in California for almost two weeks. We drove up the Pacific Coast Highway along the gorgeous beaches towards my uncle's home. I hadn't seen my uncle since I was two or three years old—so over fifty years. My uncle has a beautiful farm in Oregon and grows vegetables and fruits and makes jars of jam and other jarred veggies. It's a perfect retirement life for him. He also hosts dozens of friends throughout the year and is such an amazing cook and host. I must get my love of hospitality from him. While Dad and I were there, my uncle took us on great adventures seeing some of the breathtaking sights around Oregon. If you've never been to Oregon, you should add it to your bucket list, as it is one of the most beautiful states in the United States.

On one of those adventurous days, we met up with a lady friend of my uncle's in a small college town not too far from his farm. We met at his friend's house and had a tour of her beautiful garden. She had this perfect spot to grow shiitake mushrooms, and they were thriving. His friend then took us to this enormous open air farmers' market. There were so many different kinds of produce. Interestingly, one stand had yak steaks for sale, and another had dozens of different types of mushrooms, and another had a mountain of huge, fresh carrots (seriously, the largest amount of carrots I've ever seen in my life). After we shopped and purchased some local favorites, we settled in for lunch.

Once we had placed our lunch orders, the surface chit-chatting began. My uncle's lady friend was not much for small talk, so she threw out this question: "What do you feel like you've mastered in your life?" She looked straight at my dad, who prefers conversations about weather, politics, movies, and golf. He squirmed in his seat and was noticeably uncomfortable. I jumped in to cover for him, saying, "I think I've spent most of my adult life trying to master mothering or 'momming.' My mom was the best mother she could be, but after my brother died she kind of checked out. She also did not have much of a role model growing up. After seeing generations in her family, and in my father's family, of mothers that were emotionally unavailable, alcoholic, or abusive, I decided that I did not want that for my children." I went on to talk about my four awesome adult children and their spouses, their successes, and our present close relationships.

It was out of that conversation that God began stirring the idea of this book inside of me. He had told me years before that He wanted me to write. I had already written some drafts in the direction that I felt I had the most experience in—servanthood—but they kept falling flat. For me, nudgings from God often come in the form of a lack of peace, a stuck feeling, when writing. I tend to write from my head and not my heart and anointing if I'm not following the direction that God intends. Over time, God continued nudging and letting me know that was not what *He* wanted me to write about first. God wanted me to clear some air with His women, specifically the mothers of His children. Since I have always had a passion for being a mom and for helping other moms, the journey of Momistry began.

Momistry is a crucial season of our lives devoted to God for the purpose of raising and discipling our children, whether those children are biological, adopted, step, foster, guardianship, or a young person living in your home. Perhaps you're momming as a student, or you're an entrepreneur, or maybe you are a full-time stay-at-home mom, or a doctor, or a church secretary, or a hairdresser, or a bank teller, or school teacher. Regardless of your employment position, your most important ministry focus is fiercely raising children—children who love and serve Jesus and children who love their families. All while keeping them safe: body, soul, and spirit. Raising humans who can be self-sufficient adults contributing salt and light to their communities and, in time, raising their own children to love and serve Jesus and to love their families—that, my friends, is Momistry.

Let me give you some backstory. When Jesus first rescued me, I was a single mom and a total trainwreck. I already had two children at the time, an eight-year-old son and a four-year-old daughter. After my spiritual eyes were opened, all I wanted to do was protect them from the hurt and tragedies I had experienced growing up. It took several years for me to work on being vulnerable and emotionally available to them. Decades of self-protection had created some extremely unhealthy patterns and walls around my heart, even towards my children. God directed me to people, books, and other resources to help me learn some of the parenting and life skills I needed in order to not

> **If we grew up using self-protective tools in relationships, then unless we learn tools of connection, we will end up recreating the same broken relational dynamics we experienced growing up.**
> —Danny Silk

perpetuate the destructive generational ways of life in which I was raised.

**Hurting people, hurt people.**
**—Author Unknown**

As I was on this quest for a new life for me and my children, God brought me a husband who loved God and his family (and he still does to this day). My husband also had a child from a previous marriage, a four-year-old son. In his book *Loving our Kids on Purpose*, Danny Silk says, "If we grew up using self-protective tools in relationships, then unless we learn tools of connection, we will end up recreating the same broken relational dynamics we experienced growing up." Life is a journey, and you can follow the paths of your family or others—or you can blaze a new trail. I was determined to blaze a new trail.

Some parents who have not walked through healing from Jesus (and maybe even some therapy too) will bring the hurts that they had in their childhood into their marriages and in turn into their families. My mom and dad had difficult childhoods, and they never experienced healing from those deep wounds. Thus, they brought that hurt into raising me and my brothers. Mom received a lot of physical healing from Jesus, but I think maybe she held onto some of the harsh realities and trauma of her childhood—or perhaps stuffed them. My aunts and I would joke about my mom "living in a fairytale land." That old saying about sweeping things under the rug? Well, Mom and Dad both had pretty lumpy carpets if you know what I mean, and my dad still lives that way today.

This is why I chose to allow Jesus into those dark places in my soul. He lights up the darkness. I also walked through years of counseling and mentoring. By no means have I arrived, but after receiving healing and forgiving everyone, my journey in Momistry was deliberate and focused.

We all need help sometimes, so don't be afraid to ask. Hold on tightly to hope as you pursue healing. It's absolutely worth it!

Ladies, this was a long process of letting God's light shine in every area of my heart and soul. I was thirty years old when Jesus saved me, and I had been dragging around this internal footlocker full of junk for decades. I joke, "People say everyone has baggage when they get married. Most have a cute overnight bag or a sporty gym bag. I had an old beat-up steam trunk from World War II." It was difficult and painful but necessary work. I would do it all again. If you're interested in hearing about all the yuck from my past, you can watch one of my testimony videos on Facebook; I'll put a link in the resources. The junk that was in my trunk no longer has any power over me, and I'm not giving it any space in this book. When I say "Jesus rescued and Jesus saved me," I mean every word. If you need a season of counseling or therapy and healing to be better equipped for your Momistry, do it. I sure did.

> **We believe that the triumph of His victory is greater than the struggle of our reality.**
> **—Lisa Bevere**

God did not rescue me so I could simply go to heaven when I die. He rescued me to be filled with His presence and live life abundantly now. *"The Spirit of God, who raised Jesus from the dead, lives in you. And just as God raised Christ Jesus from the dead, he will give life to your mortal bodies by this same Spirit living within you." (Romans 8:11) "The thief's purpose is to steal and kill and destroy. My purpose is to give them a rich and satisfying life." (John 10:10)* The goal was to bring His life-giving power to my family and then to others. I knew I could not neglect the love and care my children needed. We didn't have podcasts and live streaming back then, so it was books, radio talk shows, and a few cassette tape series. While listening to radio talk shows, I would take pages of notes, highlight books, and dog-ear pages. Over time, a few people came into my life, people I could go to and seek counsel from for my Momistry journey. God's way is for younger men and women to learn from the older ones (see Titus 2:3).

I remember one time years ago when my husband and I were driving back from dropping off our children. Being a blended family, the every weekend shuffle was real for us. It was every single weekend, since I have children from a former spouse and so does my husband. We were transporting children every weekend. Yes—every weekend; it was a lot. During the drive home we were listening to a radio talk show. I cannot recall which one, but we did this frequently. We were vigilantly in training mode to learn to parent God's way. The guest on the radio show was encouraging parents to have discussions ahead of time to avoid overreacting when children stumble. My reaction simply to the suggestion of my children stumbling was contemptuous. I was a young mom assuming my kids would never skip school, smoke, watch porn (or even rated R movies for that matter), masturbate, drink or do drugs, get/make someone pregnant out of wedlock, or get arrested. "Oh my word! Those hosts are out of their minds," I thought. I mean come on, guys. I had given up my career and personal life goals to focus on Momistry and break some crazy family patterns. Our lives would be holy, utopic, and only dwell on the straight and narrow path. I thought it was foolish to talk about those things.

Well, my wise and sometimes frustrating husband felt like it was good advice, so we talked through each one of the topics. I let him take the pornography and masturbation topics. I was *not* ready to think about that, as our children were still in elementary school. Needless to say, a few of those preemptive conversations ended up being quite helpful as the years progressed. There was a lot of untraining of my assumptions regarding what things were going to look like that needed to be done in my life.

Some people that my husband and I took counsel from early on had a couple of older children serving God, so all appeared replicable. Years later their adult children shared that their parents were very harsh at home. Some of the things the children said could have maybe even been considered abuse. I'm not sure that any of their children are loving or serving God anymore. I honestly have no clue. A family that was once portrayed as a beacon of hope for those of us looking for guidance is now in much need of reconciliation and restoration from Jesus. It is so heartbreaking. Do you know what else is heartbreaking? We took some, even most, of their disciplining techniques and applied them to our children. This lesson we learned the hard way. I cannot emphasize enough the importance of listening to parenting advice from parents who all (or most) of their children are grown adults, have moved out, and are consistently bearing good fruit.

Sorting out parenting is complicated. Following someone's trail is easier than blazing your own. I knew that I didn't want to parent the way I was parented. I also knew I didn't want to parent religiously and oppressively, like how the Egyptians treated the Israelites in Exodus 5, and "have my children making bricks without straw as a harsh taskmaster." I wanted to begin momming from a place of love and mercy. *"If you want to change the world, go home and love your family."* (Mother Teresa) I needed to learn to *love* my family. That took time, prayer, patience, and a *lot* of behavior modification.

Pastor Diana, whom I introduced in my acknowledgements, once taught me: "Patty, you have to stop this pattern of reacting to everything. Take some time, and let the Holy Spirit guide you in proper responses." Yep, that was life-changing for my Momistry. I didn't, and still don't always, handle things perfectly, but it is no longer reactionary in the volatile and explosive way I was raised. I need the help of the Holy Spirit every single day. I needed Him then and still need Him today.

When the children were younger, I was a yeller and harsh disciplinarian. This was me using the dysfunctional tools I was raised with to try and control, instead of teaching. One time our eldest son mouthed off to me one too many times. We were in the car getting ready to leave for church. I jumped out of the car, opened his car door, grabbed him by the ear, and took him back into the house. He was several inches taller than me, so it was quite the sight to see. I propped him against the wall and yelled and berated him for several minutes. That's embarrassing to share, but these were the behaviors that pushed me into actively pursuing my Momistry.

In that same season of life, I had another "dysfunctional tool" moment. The children still poke at me about this one. It was well over twenty years ago. One of the kids had gotten into trouble with their dad. I was trying to persuade the child to go another direction with their attitude and disposition, but he just kept on. I tried to convince my husband to let it go. It was after dinner, and we were all settled around the TV to watch *Walker Texas Ranger* (the original, with Chuck Norris). Each of us had a bowl of ice cream. Neither my child nor my spouse were allowing my controlling behaviors to diffuse the situation. Our son mouthed off, my husband firmly corrected him, and I threw my ice cream bowl at my husband, missing and striking the wall. I then said something not very Jesus-like and stormed out of the room. I was a hot mess and needed new parenting tools.

I cringe as I type this, remembering how hard we were on our oldest son. Thankfully he is a forgiving man and knows that we were trying to do our

> **If you want to change the world, go home and love your family.**
> —**Mother Teresa**

best. There is so much truth in the fact that, as parents, most of us are just trying to do our best. We did apologize to him and ask for his forgiveness. We have apologized to all four of our adult children. I thank Jesus for rescue, reconciliation, and restoration in our family.

Being a mother in today's culture can be overwhelming, as there are many pulls, opinions, and concerns. We don't like to say "fear" if we are Christians, because we are not supposed to have fear, but the truth is that most of the moms I've talked with over the last decade have had some real fear. We have to get new tools for our Momistry to be successful. Our children need us to, our spouses need us to, and the Kingdom of God needs us to. I'm not the bright lipstick, Starbucks-in-hand, skinny jeans (I wish), social-media-face kind of mother and now grandmother. Motherhood is hard. Remember my famous slogan: "Momming is the best job ever and the hardest job ever. YOU CAN DO IT!"

While in our Momistry, we need to be filled with the Holy Spirit. I don't know how people live life without being filled with Him. With the Holy Spirit, we get out our knee pads for praying. We study God's word and His ways. Our strong lungs are ready for worshiping through battles. We intentionally partner with God to plan a course that protects our children from every plot of the enemy, protecting their body, soul, and spirit. What God says is more powerful than anything from today's culture. *"History merely repeats itself. It has all been done before. Nothing under the sun is truly new." (Ecclesiastes 1:9)*

Mommas, that is the absolute truth. We fight for the future of these children of God. They are His, and He gave them to us on purpose, for *His* purpose. We must steward them well, as He has a purpose for each one of them. Part of Momistry is us equipping them for their destiny in God. It may not look like what we expected, but children belong to God, and they are only ours to steward for a season.

> **Children are not a distraction from more important work. They are the most important work. —Anonymous**

When you have children, selfish living ends—or at least it should. We are no longer living for our dreams or desires; we are living to raise the future of the Kingdom of the Living God. "Each child is so precious in His sight," as the song says.

Throughout the upcoming chapters, we are going to address some of the questions that countless women have posed to me within the last several years. As mentioned in the introduction, we did a survey of hundreds of moms and moms-to-be asking for anonymous transparency regarding their fears (there, I said it) about mothering. My oldest is in his thirties, so we barely had the internet and cell phones when he was born. Our twelve-year-old daughter, whom we adopted in 2020, faces a whole different world than our oldest did.

Moms, the struggle and the fight is real! We have to keep our children safe: body, soul, and spirit. For that we *need* the Holy Spirit. Momistry is war! Take a deep breath, take three, and let them out slowly. (No, really, stop and take those breaths.) It's a fight to raise children who love God into their adulthood. For me, I didn't care if they became doctors, lawyers, football stars, olympic gymnastics, or famous musicians if they were going to hell in the process. *"For even if you were to gain all the wealth and power of this world with everything it could offer you—at the cost of your own life—what good would that be? And what could be more valuable to you than your own soul?" (Matthew 16:26 TPT)* *"Train up a child in the way he should go, and when he is old he will not depart from it." (Proverbs 22:6 NKJV)* It's about training in the things of God, not in education, career, sports, or finding a spouse. Those things are important, but they are not vital. God wants us to make disciples, and that starts at the kitchen table, on the sofa, and at their bedsides.

> **Physical training is good, but training for godliness is much better, promising benefits in this life and in the life to come.**
> **—1 Timothy 4:8**

If you're not filled with the Holy Spirit, or maybe you don't feel His counsel, I've added a prayer at the end of this chapter for you. Pray out loud, this helps with building your faith. *"So then faith comes by hearing, and hearing by the word of God." (Romans 10:17 NKJV)* Maybe you struggle with this part of the Trinity: Father, Son, and *Holy Spirit*. Here are a few verses to meditate on:

> *"But in fact, it is best for you that I go away, because if I don't, the Advocate won't come. If I do go away, then I will send him to you. And when he comes, he will convict the world of its sin, and of God's righteousness, and of the coming judgment. The world's sin is that it refuses to believe in me. Righteousness is available because*

*I go to the Father, and you will see me no more. Judgment will come because the ruler of this world has already been judged. There is so much more I want to tell you, but you can't bear it now. When the Spirit of truth comes, he will guide you into all truth. He will not speak on his own but will tell you what he has heard. He will tell you about the future." (John 16:7-13)*

*"So if you sinful people know how to give good gifts to your children, how much more will your heavenly Father give the Holy Spirit to those who ask him?" (Luke 11:13)*

*"And God has given us his Spirit as proof that we live in him and he in us." (1 John 4:13)*

*"I baptize with water those who repent of their sins and turn to God. But someone is coming soon who is greater than I am—so much greater that I'm not worthy even to be his slave and carry his sandals. He will baptize you with the Holy Spirit and with fire." (Matthew 3:11)*

Take a few minutes and ask the Holy Spirit to show you areas where you know you need help. Or, ask Him to show you any "blindspots"; these are areas you need help, but they are familiar to you so you don't see them anymore. A quick example is reacting instead of responding, as I mentioned earlier. Knee-jerk reactions were what was familiar to me. I'm so thankful that God brought an amazing couple into my life while I was looking for

**So then faith comes by hearing, and hearing by the word of God.**
**—Romans 10:17 NKJV**

parenting guidance. It's so helpful to have that support throughout the seasons of life.

Let's make disciples. "Your most important disciples are sitting at your kitchen table." (Toby Mack, Speak Life) Together we can raise world changers. I'm praying for you. I'm cheering for you. May the journey of starting your Momistry begin NOW!

**Momming is the best job ever and the hardest job ever. YOU CAN DO IT!**

# **Prayers:**

Here is a prayer for you to say out loud to receive the Holy Spirit: *Jesus, I thank You for sending the Holy Spirit to guide and counsel me. I don't always feel Him inside of me, and I want every good gift You paid full price on the cross to give. You have given us the Holy Spirit. I pray right now that You would baptize me and fill me with Your Holy Spirit so I may discern Your will and clearly follow His leading. Awaken anything in me that is not listening to Your voice. I need Your Holy Spirit, and I surrender my ways and embrace the Holy Spirit, who is truth. In the name of Jesus, AMEN.*

Here is another prayer for you to say out loud: *God, I love You. Thank You for the life You have given me. May I see all of Your goodness and blessings. Father, I thank You for these children that You have entrusted me with. I want to raise them to love and serve You and then do the same for their children and grandchildren unto a thousand generations. Help me to open my heart wide to Your Holy Spirit. I invite the Holy Spirit to show me any areas of my heart that need healing. Expose any behaviors or reactions that I may have to Your glorious light. I do not take parenting lightly, and I submit my children and my Momistry to You. Thank You for new mercies every day. Thank You, Jesus, for new hope and new life. Empower me by Your Holy Spirit to be all that You've called me to be. Amen.*

## Practical points and questions:

1. What are some good traits from your family growing up that you would like to incorporate into your new family?
2. Are you learning and growing in your "Momistry" using different resources? If so, what are they?
3. What are some negative family patterns that you do not want to repeat?
4. Do you react from your emotions or respond from the Holy Spirit?
5. Have you parented harshly or religiously, and do you need to apologize to your spouse and children and start fresh?
6. Write what the Holy Spirit is speaking to you. For those who are new to being filled with the Holy Spirit, you can hear Him in many different ways, such as Scriptures that stand out or a word you feel sweet and strong in your spirit or heart. Another way is when you are singing, praying, or writing and something comes out of your mouth and you have no idea where it came from. Yes, it's HIM! There is no right or wrong answer when writing. This is a good time to clear out the clutter of thoughts by writing them down.

# Notes:

# CHAPTER 2

# Be FREE to be a Momma Bear

> ```
> There is no greater warrior
> than  a  mother  protecting
> her child.
> ```
>
> N. K. Jemisin

When I started taking this Momistry thing seriously, I wanted to keep my children safe: body, soul, and spirit. I remember numerous times being told that I was a "momma bear." It was often said in a condescending tone, as if it were a bad thing. This didn't happen just once from one person; it was numerous times by other moms, friends, family, teachers, leaders, and even pastors. Usually they were women who were slightly older than I and seemed more experienced at this whole parenting thing. While maybe they thought being a momma bear was negative, I eventually realized it wasn't; knowing there is a real enemy that wants to steal, kill, and destroy (see John 10:10) is critical. Having had such a hard childhood, I knew the enemy all too well and wanted to do what I could to protect my children from the tragedies of my past and from the enemy of our souls. At first, I struggled to develop a healthy filter regarding the phrase "momma bear."

I grew up in a day where you played outside until the streetlights came on. Back in the day, we had sleepovers without much supervision, vast neighborhoods to roam, old beat-up bikes to ride, and, when bored, rocks to throw. I laugh now about the scar I still have on top of my head from a rock fight when I was ten or eleven years old. Left unattended next to a large parking lot and surrounded by a six-foot-tall, long chain link fence with an apartment complex next door created a perfect environment for trouble, especially late in the summer and just past eight o'clock at night. The group of kids I was with began taunting another group of kids on the other side of the fence. I'm not really sure who started what, but not too long after the name calling came the rock throwing. Long story short, I ended up with five stitches and a bald spot on my big blonde head.

My mom was not a momma bear and wasn't much of a protector in general, mainly because she was always working to make sure we had food. She had a way of marrying unstable men that didn't have steady work, except my father whom she divorced when I was 4. Mom was busy keeping food on the table and the lights on (most of the time) and wasn't protective at all, so I had no baseline for protecting my children as a parent. To Mom's defense, we didn't have as much kidnapping, murder, sex trafficking, and crazy online dangers like we do today. It is so important today for you to be free to be a momma bear for your children. I believe it is more important now than any other time in history.

Being a momma bear in your Momistry is doing whatever is necessary to keep our children safe: body, soul, and spirit. You may grow weary of hearing me say this, but it's imperative to establish a routine of saying to yourself and to your children, "My Momistry is to keep my children safe." In order to do that, at times we will all have to be momma bears. The only thing that may cause you to stumble in this area is if you struggle with pleasing people or wrestle with the fear of man. Keeping your Momistry a priority will help you say and do hard things (with love) and stand firmly while protecting your human cubs. Remember to be slow to respond and not to react. Take time to listen to the Holy Spirit. Start telling your children that your job is to keep them safe, and then continue telling them that for a hundred years or until you die, whichever comes first.

Momma Bears:

- <u>We pray fervently:</u> *"The earnest prayer of a righteous person has great power and produces wonderful results." (James 5:16)*
- <u>We listen to the Holy Spirit:</u> *"When the Spirit of truth comes, he will guide you into all truth. He will not speak on his own but will tell you what he has heard. He will tell you about the future." (John 16:13)*
- <u>We speak:</u> *"The Spirit of the Lord is on me, because he has anointed me to proclaim good news to the poor. He has sent me to proclaim freedom for the prisoners and recovery of sight for the blind, to set the oppressed free." (Luke 4:18)*
- <u>We are strong and fight fiercely:</u> *"A final word: Be strong in the Lord and in his mighty power. Put on all of God's armor so that you will be able to stand firm against all strategies of the devil. For we are not fighting against flesh-and-blood enemies, but against evil rulers and authorities of the unseen world, against mighty powers in this dark world, and against evil spirits in the heavenly places." (Ephesians 6:10-12)*
- <u>We love unconditionally:</u> *"Love is patient and kind. Love is not jealous or boastful or proud or rude. It does not demand its own way. It is not irritable, and it keeps no record of being wronged. It does not rejoice about injustice but rejoices whenever the truth wins out. Love never gives up, never loses faith, is always hopeful, and endures through every circumstance." (1 Corinthians 13:4-7)*
- <u>We teach and train:</u> *"And these words which I command you today shall be in your heart. You shall teach them diligently to your children, and shall talk of them when you sit in your house, when you*

*walk by the way, when you lie down, and when you rise up." (Deuteronomy 6:6-7 NKJV) "Train up a child in the way he should go, and when he is old he will not depart from it." (Proverbs 22:6 NKJV)*

- <u>We set an example:</u> *"Don't let anyone think less of you because you are young. Be an example to all believers in what you say, in the way you live, in your love, your faith, and your purity." (1 Timothy 4:12)*
- <u>We are always on alert:</u> *"Stay alert! Watch out for your great enemy, the devil. He prowls around like a roaring lion, looking for someone to devour." (1 Peter 5:8)*

As momma bears, there will be many times that you have to pray, and all you can do is pray and trust God. Other times, the Holy Spirit will wake you up and nudge you to check your child's phone, their backpack, their bedroom, their grades, the history on their computer, etc. We have to listen to and obey those nudges. When people are being downright ungodly and/or unsafe, you will have to grab the strength of the Holy Spirit and boldly speak out. Momistry is a fierce battle, and we must fight for the destinies of our children. We run into the spiritual battlefield to push back against "evil spirits in heavenly places" (see Ephesians 6:12).

As part of loving our children unconditionally, we never withhold love as a consequence. Momma bears *always* love their cubs, no matter what they've said or done. This doesn't mean we always have to like them, but we do always have to love them. Night and day we teach and train our kiddos the Word of God—His ways and not our ways. Our children are watching what we say and how we act, so we must be people of faith, purity, and love. This last one is so important: We are *alert*. There is an enemy looking to devour our children (see 1 Peter 5:8).

One time when my oldest daughter was in second grade, she came home from school with a disturbing new assignment. The teacher was reading a popular book about witchcraft to the classroom. I was a young and overzealous (religious) new Christian, so I immediately contacted the teacher (reacting not responding). She dismissed my concern, justifying that the book was approved by the administration. She offered no solution other than my daughter being forced to sit and listen to a glorification of something our God hated, witchcraft (see Leviticus 19:26, Deuteronomy 18:10, Revelation 21:8).

> **We run into the spiritual battlefield to push back against "evil spirits in heavenly places."**

Instead of me coaching my daughter through the information in the book, and explaining that it was considered to be just entertainment by some, I reached out to the school administration. My daughter was (and still is) filled with the Holy Spirit and was grieved, as were a couple of other classmates of hers. The administration offered the solution of the girls going to the office and sitting with the secretary during reading; however, only my daughter took the stand. The school secretary gave her candy, and she read a book of her choosing quietly in the secretary's office.

Our daughter was young and stood up for what was right. However, seven years old is too young to have to take the persecution of teasing from other classmates and some disdain from her teacher. In hindsight, I wish I'd guided her through the content and helped her pray for her classmates and teacher. Keeping her spirit safe was my goal. I'd rather err on the side of over-protecting than under-protecting 100% of the time. Sometimes you will make wrong decisions, but if your motive is keeping them safe, that's a good start. If I'd taken time and prayed and given this some thought, I may have handled it in a healthier way. My daughter is thirty now and jokes with me about "scarring her for life." I was a bit of a reckless momma bear back them, reacting and not responding. It's a little embarrassing now to look back on, and my goal is to help you learn from my mistakes.

When my oldest son was in sixth grade, he was stabbed in the leg with a dart by a student that was being reintegrated into the classroom. This much larger child continued to bully my son, so I had to contact school administration again (same school). The teacher's hands were tied, as it seemed more important for the student doing the bullying to stay in class. The boy was never given consequences for stabbing someone with a dart. His bullying and intimidation of fellow classmates was also tolerated, of course with constant attempts at redirection. After over a month of talking to the school and continuous battles with this issue, praying and trying not to react, we decided to try our hand at homeschooling. We felt led by peace that God wanted us to make the sacrifices necessary to homeschool. This was new to us since my husband and I were both public school students. As a momma bear, I needed to keep my cubs a little closer for a season, so they could be and feel safe. Being safe and feeling safe are not the same thing; lack of either one can be harmful to their bodies, souls, and/or spirits.

For the purpose of safety, we homeschooled for a few years. I enjoyed that time with the kids. It was difficult, and some days school just didn't happen, but we made a lot of great life memories. Be prepared to do whatever you have to do to keep your children safe: body, soul, and spirit. Sometimes it will be wrong, like my second-grade daughter and the book. With her I was totally going off my own emotion, not the prompting of the Holy Spirit. Other times it will be right and feel right. Also, it can be right and not feel good at all. Be led by peace. *"The peace that Christ gives is to guide you in the decisions you make; for it is to this peace that God has called you together in the one body. And be thankful."* (*Colossians 3:15 GNT)*

I don't use the Good News Translation very often, but it's verbage for Colossians 3:15 clearly made the point. Being led by peace is the "knowing" in your spirit that what you're doing is right. Sometimes it's the Holy Spirit clearly giving you peace inside your heart. Other times, it's knowing what God says about the situation, and you have peace trusting in His word. It may feel scary in your emotions/soul and be peaceful in your spirit. Sometimes you will still get it wrong, because we are momma bears! Just like when the disciple cut the guy's ear off, which was not what Jesus wanted (see Luke 22:50-51), God has grace on us as we learn to walk this out. Have grace on yourself and others, too.

Be patient as you grow and learn as a momma bear; I handled conflicts with bullies very differently with our youngest son than I did with our eldest son, after I had years in Momistry under my belt. One time when our youngest son was in sixth grade, he was in a private school and had a few run-ins with a bully classmate. I told him, "If he does it again, you warn him once and then clean his clock. I will deal with the school." Boy, that one did not feel right, but it was right. "Turn the other cheek" was screaming in my ear; however, there was perfect peace in my spirit. My son had already talked to the teacher numerous times. The next time the bully shoved my son, he firmly and verbally set clear boundaries. The kid shoved my son again, and he enforced those boundaries physically. Sure, my son ended up in the principal's office. He did not get consequences that day, but he did get respect. From that day on, there were no more issues with that bully. Interestingly, the two boys actually became pretty good friends in high school.

There are times as a momma bear when you stand up for your children; then there are times when you coach them through standing up for themselves. Please note that when we took our eldest son and daughter out of school to homeschool, it was primarily for protection. As parents, it is our job to train up a child, but in order to do that we must understand the importance of being a momma bear and keeping them safe: body, soul, and spirit. Bullying can do damage not only to the body but also to the soul and spirit, so be a momma bear if you need to. Listen, if I can homeschool for a season, anyone can. There's so much help online with support groups and such nowadays. Some public schools are a whirlwind of chaos and confusion, and some are not. We need the Holy Spirit on this topic for sure. Remember to always be led by peace.

You can ask any of my children, "What's your mom's job?" and they will all reply, "Her job is to keep me safe." Our youngest two will certainly answer that way. Sometimes I feel bad for our older children. There were way too many trial and error moments for them. Hopefully, you mommas don't repeat some of our mistakes. Trying to find examples of what a healthy momma bear looks like is difficult. Some moms

> **Being safe and feeling safe are not the same thing; lack of either one can be harmful to their bodies, souls, and/or spirits.**

are helicopter moms: controlling, overprotective, fearful, worrisome, smothering, and never let their children out of their sight. Then other moms are more like hippies: they are super carefree and say "Just do whatever you want" and are too busy to be bothered. Mommas, it's our responsibility to keep our children safe and to be actively training them in the things of God. We are not hippies or helicopters; we are MOMMA BEARS!

A young mother was sharing with me recently about taking some kids to the park. She runs a daycare in her home and has a couple of young children of her own. It was a beautiful spring day in Missouri, and the park was full. After several weeks of rain, the Midwest kids all had cabin fever. While her crew was playing at the park, her oldest son began climbing a tree. A couple of other kids at the park started to as well. When the other children's moms saw them, they bolted over and scolded them for climbing the dangerous tree. As they dragged their children away, they gave harsh, judgemental dirty looks to my friend. If you're already a mom, you know exactly the looks I'm talking about. My friend's child is a boy. He and his other brothers climb trees, ride bikes, build forts, wrestle, and play football, because they are boys. She was standing six feet from the tree with her other kids playing on the playground equipment close by. She was being a momma bear by letting her son learn confidence, gain skills, and build strength, as well as get out some boy juice. Children, and even adults, learn by playing safely where it is dangerous. A helicopter mom grabs her child and keeps them out of *any* possible danger. Life is full of danger, and sometimes a broken arm builds endurance. We must trust that we know what is safe for our children. That's why God gave them to us.

In the survey we did with moms and moms-to-be, a concern we listed as an option was, "How will I protect my children from bullies, accidents, failing, etc...?" This was a major concern for 64% of the hundreds of women surveyed. My answer for this is: "You really can't, always." God is in control; we are not. Momma bears teach their cubs to survive and thrive on their own so they can be self-sufficient, independent adults. Helicopter moms overprotect, overprovide, and most of the time end up raising dependent, entitled adults who need others to provide for them, and sometimes those children live in their parents' basement until they're 30. Hippie moms can't be bothered, so their children become rebellious and wild. These children often grow up to be criminals.

**Momma bears teach their cubs to survive and thrive on their own so they can be self-sufficient, independent adults.**

As children grow, you must allow them to fail, make wrong choices, and learn. This is part of life. They learn serious life lessons in the safety of our home and care. We teach them to fail with honor, to have accidents and make things right, and to learn to pay the consequences for wrong choices. We walk them and talk them through it, all of it.

On the topic of bullying, you will have to make that choice with your children in each situation. Do we encourage them to walk away, stand up, or help someone out? Most of the confrontations that my eldest daughter had in high school were her standing up to someone bullying one of her friends. Most of the time when the bullying was toward her, she would walk away. Mommas, the truth is there will be bullies and mean girls, but there will be bullies and mean girls in our adult lives too, and we must teach our children what to do and when to do it. This includes online bullying as well. Teach and pray. Ask the Holy Spirit to give you wisdom and discernment, and He will.

I shared our bully experiences with our sons a few paragraphs ago. There are dozens of mean girl stories I could share. If you have daughters, prepare yourself for hours of conversations and training on how to be kind and what kindness looks like, how to respond to snarky comments and when not to respond. Again, teach and pray, pray, pray.

When our eldest daughter was in high school, she sang in the choir. There was a girl in the choir who was known for pushing people around and bullying. One day she was saying something rude to my daughter, and my daughter just ignored her and went to walk away. This girl proceeded to smack my daughter in the face. My daughter braced herself and shoved the girl, and the girl fell down the choir risers, and the classmates began cheering. The bully got up, and my daughter squared off, glared at her, and through clenched teeth said, "Girl, I have three brothers. I am not afraid of you." The girl turned to her friends and walked away. Throughout the whole day at school, students our daughter didn't even know came up to her and thanked her. Sometimes standing up to a mean girl is for others more than it is for yourself.

Bullying is not always physical for mean girls. Bullying can be gossip, slander, lies, manipulation, put downs, control, or threats. It can be notes in lockers and lies about grades—or, worse, sexual activity. Remember that our Momistry as momma bears is to keep them safe: body, soul, and spirit. It's to keep them safe no matter what that looks like.

Mean girls are the real deal, especially when girls are ages ten through seventeen. Make sure you're talking to your daughters about this early on, maybe even in early elementary school. I've worked with mean girls. A young mom was asking me for help the other day in reference to a "friend" of hers. These ladies are in their late twenties, yet her friend was still a gossip, manipulator, backstabber, and well, honestly, a narcissist. We have to love people, but we do not have to share our lives with perpetually mean people. Adults that act like teenagers are toxic. Teach your daughters young, and teach them well. Teach and pray.

Listen, I get it. It's difficult. The sleepless nights, the fights with our spouses, the never-ending laundry and dishes, having to choose and prepare meals: It's difficult. It's exhausting. I once saw a meme that said, "No one ever told me I would make so many sandwiches as an adult." It's true. You're feeding humans who want three meals a day. With babies, there are bottles, pumps, and germs, and with first babies, there's learning how to change a diaper in the dark or remembering to leave a night light on or to take toys for entertainment when visiting others.

Back in the day, we had to boil the bottles to sterilize them; there was no dishwashing. We didn't have bottle warmers, wipe warmers, or sound machines other than a bathroom or box fan. We also used baby powder and had bumper sets on the crib. Think of how much things will change by the time your children are parents. It's quite the quandary how it's sometimes easier to protect them from unseen germs than it is from seen things. With Germ X, bleach, essential oils, washing machines, and dishwashers, germ-killing has sure gotten easier. But being a momma bear isn't about protecting our kids from scrapes, failures, or even germs. It's not about putting them in a bubble or forcing them into perfect behavior. It's about being alert for the spiritual and physical threats that want to harm them. We must be alert, momma bears! *"Stay alert! Watch out for your great enemy, the devil. He prowls around like a roaring lion, looking for someone to devour." (1 Peter 5:8)*

A pastor once said, "Keep your children closer as teens; that's when they need you the most." We think that as babies they are so needy, and they certainly are in terms of physical sustenance. As tweens and teens, they need our wisdom and discernment and to hear our life experiences so they can avoid making life-altering poor choices. They need guidance on how to make the right choices and have the right friends.

When my children were teens, I told them about my past. They learned about my life before Jesus. They knew I drank, did drugs, and was promiscuous. I told them how empty and dark and lonely it was. They could come and talk to me about anything at any time of day or night. Listen, if our kids aren't talking to us, they are talking to someone. I always wanted to be their safe place. You have to invest time into connecting with your children when they are young if you want to be their safe place when they are tweens and teens. It doesn't come from one conversation; it comes from hundreds.

It took a lot of self-sacrifice on my part, but as a momma bear their safety was my first concern. Now that they're grown, and some of them have their own children, I do not regret one sleepless night, one late night drive to pick them up, or one visit with them to a pastor for counsel. I have regrets with my firstborn, as he witnessed and was the brunt of a lot of my Momistry failures. You will fail sometimes. It's best just to repent, apologize, and move forward. You can't be an effective momma bear if you're beating yourself up for what happened the day, week, month, or even years before. Let it go, and that will help you keep your cubs close.

Not only do we have our four children and our adopted daughter, but we have also had over thirty young people live with us over the last decade. Some of those have been pastors' kids seeking healing and a fresh start. Others have been ministry school students and a few people from other countries just needing a safe place to land for a week, month, or year. As I mentioned earlier, some of the young people who lived in our home called me "Patty Mom" or "Momma Patty." Of course those that were older adults did not. I have "momma beared" a lot of people: everyone from a young girl who wanted to start dating immediately upon relocating halfway across the nation and a twenty-three-year-old man who should be working and self-sufficient but preferred not working and a home with everything provided (eventually we lovingly kicked him out of the nest). Oh, the stories I could tell. Maybe that will be another book.

**As a momma bear, I desperately needed the Holy Spirit to properly guide and direct and even discipline.**

One thing I learned from all of these sons and daughters of God is that they *all* are so very different. As a momma bear, I desperately needed the Holy Spirit to properly guide and direct and even discipline. You might not be my child by birth, but if you're living in my house and come in drunk and past curfew, you will have consequences.

We cannot compare, judge, or parent each child the same. We have to keep their differences in mind. We must be filled with the Holy Spirit to know how God would want situations handled for each unique person. *"After all, who can really see into a person's heart and know his hidden impulses except for that person's spirit? So it is with God. His thoughts and secrets are only fully understood by his Spirit, the Spirit of God."* (1

*Corinthians 2:11 TPT)* There are some tools that might help you understand your individual children better, like the Enneagrams, DISC personality tests, or love languages. Every person has their own unique identity. Each person has not just personality but past, environment, intellect, emotional maturity, trauma, physical sickness, etc. It's not "one size fits all" for parenting, nor can you solely rely on how other people are parenting. The Holy Spirit is our Helper.

Take a moment and close your eyes. Take three slow, deep breaths and pause. I pray right now that you receive the anointing from God to walk out your years as a momma bear, serving your children in your Momistry. I pray that you would have wisdom and strength and discernment from the Holy Spirit. He is faithful, willing, and able to empower you to do this. AMEN!

Not long ago when my youngest daughter was eleven, we went to the grocery store. She wanted to push the cart to help, so I let her—after of course reminding her that she would get fired from that driving job the first time she ran into me or another person. She was doing well and had been growing in her awareness of others and things while cart pushing. (Side note: If your child cannot push a grocery basket without hitting something or someone, I encourage you *not* to sign for them to get their driver's license!) As we entered the dairy section, I stepped around the corner to get some flavored coffee creamer. My daughter waited just six feet away, as the area was a bit congested (yes, all the ladies were getting their flavored, sugary indulgences for their coffee). Out of nowhere, this man in his forties wearing a badge and hospital maintenance or janitorial attire walks right up to my daughter, into her personal space, smiles big, and starts chatting with her. My momma bear and Holy Spirit radar immediately went off, and I grabbed that basket and pulled it toward me and glared at him. If my eyes had been daggers, I may have been in big trouble.

Listen, ladies, we all know the creeper spirit—or as we sometimes call it, "creeper vibe"—and if you don't, you have a Helper that does, the Holy Spirit. Trust the Holy Spirit, your mom gut, or pastors on this one; it's perverse and ugly and so cunning. I asked my daughter why she was talking to him, and she said she felt obligated to be nice and polite. I spoke some powerful freedom to her; I told her that being safe is more important than being nice. We can be kind and direct and set a firm boundary. Looking away and not replying is absolutely okay with a stranger when you're 11.

As we made our way through the store, the guy kept appearing every few aisles, looking at her and then looking away. When we got to the checkout stand, I began unloading the shopping cart on the conveyor, so I was standing by the very front of the basket. My daughter was still standing by the push handle. Out of the blue, there was this man again. He stepped right up into my daughter's personal space yet again. My claws came out. I immediately stepped right between him and my daughter and said, "You're done here." He tried to joke, and I stepped two inches closer to him, staring him straight in the eye, and through gritted teeth said, "YOU ARE DONE HERE." My kids tell me I have a mom growl. He immediately bolted away. I turned back toward the register, and the cashier and bagger were wide-eyed, staring at me with their mouths hanging open, like I was a crazy woman. I smiled big, looked them both directly in the eyes, and calmly said, "Sorry about that. My job is to keep her safe." The young lady cashier agreed and chatted quite enthusiastically throughout the rest of our checkout process about the need for safety these days. Momma bears, we're needed. Some people will sneer at you and call you overprotective, and others will cheer you on. A few will look at you like you're crazy. It doesn't matter to me; my Momistry is to keep my children safe: body, soul, and spirit.

Please note that I did take the time to stop and talk to my daughter about protecting herself by setting boundaries. As much as we want to build a twelve-foot wall around our children until they're twenty-three years old, that's just not wisdom, nor is it realistic. Teach them young so that when they go off to college or leave the nest, they have felt safety, so they know what it feels like when it is not safe and have the tools to handle the situation.

> **I think the world today is upside down, and is suffering so much, because there is so very little love in the homes and in family life.**
> **—Mother Teresa**

Feeling protective doesn't stop when your children graduate high school or even when they get married. I still pray over them and declare God's hand over all of their lives almost daily. My eldest son deployed to Iraq during wartime. My older daughter has traveled all over Europe with an educational program and has also been on a ministry trip, twice when she was under eighteen. My other two sons have traveled extensively too, all internationally without us parents. Our family travels together have only been in the United States. The kids have gone parasailing on Waikiki Beach and Chesapeake Bay, whitewater rafted the Colorado River, rode horses and ATV's, snorkeled, swam with stingrays, surfed, hiked, ziplined, and just about every risky adventure that would require fierce, motherly momma bear prayers and fasting.

Last year, our then eleven-year-old daughter went tubing behind a boat for the first time and hiked a real Ozark mountain with a cliff and swam in a lake. This year she, now twelve, rode her first roller coaster and swam in the ocean and drove a bumper car. Yep, they all survived! God has entrusted us to be guardians of these humans and to keep them safe: body, soul, and spirit. *"Now may the God of peace make you holy in every way, and may your whole spirit and soul and body be kept blameless until our Lord Jesus Christ comes again." (1 Thessalonians 5:23)*

One morning I got to go with my eldest daughter to take her firstborn to preschool for his first day. Daddy was out of town for work, and she needed help with all of the first day supplies. Mostly she needed me to chitchat all the way there about the weekend and our new flooring for the dining room. All of the feelings of dropping your child off somewhere new and different were raging. Of course it didn't help that she was five months pregnant. My grandson was almost eighteen months old. He loves people and is super adventurous and fearless. I tell him all the time, "You are strong and stable like your daddy. You will love God and serve Him all the days of your life. You will live in God's provision and will never know lack. Your hands will be filled with hope and healing to take everywhere you go." Of course his little brain doesn't quite understand that, but his little spirit man does. As a pastor friend once said, "There is no junior Holy Spirit."

**We can't fall apart in front of our children and expect them to trust us as momma bears to keep them safe.**

When we arrived at the preschool, my grandson went right in with the teacher. He was so excited with not one drop of fear. Meanwhile,

Grandma prayed for angels to encamp the building, declared that our feet were there and that this was holy ground, prayed for a hedge of protection, and spoke the blood of Jesus over every inch of ground and every worker and child there. I prayed this, because I know who the Great Protector is. I didn't make a scene and yell and stomp; God is not deaf, and neither is our enemy. The enemy knows the bloodline of Jesus.

Afterward, my daughter and I went to Starbucks. Listen, sometimes coffee and/or ice cream is what you need to help you get back to center again. As she drove, she talked about the tears and the sleepless nights. I encouraged her to "Hold it all together, and be strong in front of your son." He knew it was a safe place, because Mom and Grandma only want good for him. We can't fall apart in front of our children and expect them to trust us as momma bears to keep them safe. Girl, I'm not saying you can't have a meltdown; just do it in the bathroom or shower or in your pillow or in the car when you're alone. God made us in His image, and He is a passionate, loving Father. He knows and understands our deep love for our children. Pray, cry, scream, whatever you need to do that's legal, then trust Him. We must be strong and stable momma bears.

> **For God will never give you the spirit of fear, but the Holy Spirit who gives you mighty power, love, and self-control.**
> **—2 Timothy 1:7 TPT**

We've talked about being a safe place for our children. If we are unstable and unavailable, our children will pick up on it, and to them that is not safe. They must be able to trust that our "yes" means yes and our "no" means no. It's okay that they know you have emotions and that you know how to manage them. We teach by the example we set, so I've had to often ask myself, "What kind of example is this?" Stability is vital. Two-year-olds have meltdowns; twenty-five-year-olds do not. Or if they do it's screaming to Jesus in the bathroom with the shower running and the door closed, on a chair in a pastor's office, or on a couch in a therapist's office. If your children worry that you're going to freak out if they ask you about something, they will probably ask someone else. Stay calm. *"For God will never give you the spirit of fear, but the Holy Spirit who gives you mighty power, love, and self-control." (2 Timothy 1:7 TPT)*

Young mommas sometimes ask me which was the scariest time or season of my Momistry, and my answer unequivocally is "all of them." It's the truth. I think maybe they're hoping for a time when the concerns (fears) or thoughts stop, as if being a momma bear has a date when the contract ends. It doesn't, and it shouldn't.

Here's a recent momma bear moment from the grandma bear. My eldest daughter had her first child and had been home from the hospital for almost two weeks, and I was helping her as much as she asked for and needed. She would text me every morning what my grandchild's sleep pattern from the night before had been, how he had eaten, etc. One morning I hadn't heard from her. I texted—no reply. I texted my son-in-love—no reply. I waited an hour, called both numbers, and still no answer. I waited fifteen more minutes, tried another round of texts and calls, still nothing. My anointing is Momistry, but by trade, I'm an insurance agent, so I knew that carbon monoxide, fire, and burglars were common claims. My grandma bear concerns began.

I waited another hour, then guess what I did? Yep! They live less than two miles from me. I jumped in the car and drove over there. I have a key to the front door to help with their dog whenever needed. I got to their house, and there was no sign of fire. I knocked on the door, and there was no answer. I unlocked the door and was greeted by a very happy and alive doggy, so no carbon monoxide. I stepped out onto their back deck thinking maybe they were in the backyard. We live in Missouri, and it was August, so it's hot, and mornings and evenings are the best times to be outside. They weren't outside. As I walked back into the house, there stood my son-in-love, hair disheveled, face all scrunched, shirtless and in shorts holding a handgun in his hand. Then came smiles, laughs, apologies, and awkwardness as expected, every single bit. But do you know what? They weren't angry at all. As parents they now understood. At fifty-four years old, I was still a momma/grandma bear, and I still am today. Grandma bear is such a fun season.

> **This is my command—be strong and courageous! Do not be afraid or discouraged. For the Lord your God is with you wherever you go.**
> **—Joshua 1:9**

There will be times when you just have to go with what the Holy Spirit gives you and pray that you hear Him correctly. If you establish with your children when they are younger that all you want is good for them, then that can be their filter when you have to set boundaries and sometimes just say "no." They understand your job is to keep them safe: body, soul, and spirit.

Let me share one more story. (I've told several, and my writing coach suggests only a few stories a chapter, but I think I've exceeded that. I have thirty-four years of stories, so here goes.) When our youngest son was seven, he wanted to play football. He played with his brothers and friends and liked it and was looking for a hobby. So the next season, we signed him up for a local flag football team. When we arrived at the first night of practice, he was so excited. When the coaches saw his size and skill, they immediately moved him to the next age group, which were eight- to ten-year-olds. They were playing tackle football, not flag. The training was intense, and the older kids were harsh. My boys love to throw the football and wrestle and can play very rough, but not in a hurtful way, and teasing and cussing were never allowed. That was not what my seven-year-old signed up for. I could've played the "mom card" and simply never taken him back and been out the $300 fee and $200 worth of equipment but would have lost the opportunity for a valuable life lesson. After the third or fourth practice, I could tell my son was upset. We talked in the car on the way home, and he shared that he did not want to "give himself" to football. Instead, he was just looking for a hobby. He said he felt like the coach wanted him to live and breathe football, and he wanted to love his family and God and his friends, and this was not what he expected. I could tell he was hurting but let him make the decision and walked with him through it. Sometimes things are not what you think, especially at seven.

The next night we went to practice, and he told the coach he was quitting. I was standing there to make sure he was well-covered, his momma bear right by his side. He looked the coach straight in the eye and told him that football was his hobby and not his life. The coach gave him the quitter speech, and I sent my son to the car. The coach began berating me for allowing my son to be a quitter and said that if he starts quitting now he won't get anywhere in life. I smiled (through gritted teeth) and kindly reminded the coach he was seven and that we had a long way to go to work that out. Looking back, I wish I'd kept in contact with that coach, so he could see the children's social media following my son created when he was twelve called Kids4the1God and the album *Mighty King* which he wrote all of the songs for. He produced it, and it was on all music platforms, as well as available on CD, all when he was sixteen. Also, he graduated valedictorian and was Student of the Year two years in a row in high school. He graduated college with a ministry degree and is a youth leader at our church. He's a successful entrepreneur and started his own business at twenty-three. Mommas, it's okay to allow our children to make mistakes, even $500 mistakes. What a valuable life lesson we talked and walked through. We prayed and canceled the words spoken by that coach. He had no authority to speak over my son's life. Keeping our children covered is so important.

Our Momistry is to keep our children safe: body, soul, and spirit. While my son was not in any physical danger, he was in emotional and spiritual danger. Words are powerful, and my job is to keep him safe. Spoken words can be damaging, especially those from stupid adults. My eldest daughter has just recently received healing from some very hurtful words spoken over her by church leaders (not pastors) over ten years ago. With that healing came new freedom. Words are powerful; they should always bring life and hope. As momma bears, be ready to counter any words spoken over your children with truth. Also, if you have had words spoken over you from a parent or someone that was a leader, like my daughter had, let those words go. It's never too late to receive healing. After you let them go, those words no longer have any power over you. Be free to be a momma bear. Ladies, keep your cubs and any cubs God brings into your life SAFE!

Remember, being a momma bear is a battle. So be strong and courageous. *"Not by might nor by power, but by my Spirit,' says the Lord Almighty." (Zechariah*

**Keeping our children covered is so important.**

*4:6 NIV)* Our strength comes from the Lord, not us. So be strong and courageous. Don't shrink back from the fear of man or pressure from others or even culture. Listen, if Jesus can flip tables and take a whip (see John 2:15) to vendors in the "foyer of the synagogue" (my paraphrase) and also pull little children up on His lap, we too can be led by the Spirit to protect and defend. No matter what it looks like. These children are your cubs; God gave them to *you* for your Momistry.

## Momming is the best job ever and the hardest job ever. YOU CAN DO IT!

## Prayer:

Pray this prayer out loud: *Thank You, God, for Your goodness. You have blessed me with these children, and I take my role as a momma bear very seriously. Holy Spirit, help me to be bold and wise. Please give me discernment in each situation. I fear the Lord, not man. Give me courage and supernatural strength to raise my children to love You and to love their families. I pray the blood of Jesus over my children to protect them. Help me, God, in my Momistry to keep them safe: body, soul, and spirit. Amen!*

# Practical points and questions:

1. Listen to the Holy Spirit for wisdom and discernment. Ask God for His wisdom on being a momma bear. Write down what you hear from Him or what's in your heart in the notes portion below. Remember, it's a place to clear your thoughts, and that's helpful when listening to God. *"If you need wisdom, ask our generous God, and he will give it to you. He will not rebuke you for asking." (James 1:5)*
2. Stay alert to what's going on in your child's life: body, soul, and spirit.
3. Remember that your job is to keep them safe and to train them and guide them.
4. Do not compare your children to each other or to other children. Every human has a unique stamp from God from when they were in the womb *"You made all the delicate, inner parts of my body and knit me together in my mother's womb." (Psalms 139:13)*
5. Be strong and courageous! God will back you up when you are protecting your children, which is not the same as controlling, so listen to Him for help.
6. It's okay to say "yes," and it's okay to say "no." Be free!
7. In what areas do you need work to become a strong and courageous momma bear?
8. Where are you doing well as a momma bear? Celebrate your successes!

# Notes:

# CHAPTER 3

## Find a Mentor and Fill Your Toolbelt

> The delicate balance of mentoring someone is not creating them in your own image, but giving them the opportunity to create themselves.
>
> Steven Spielberg

Of all the suggestions I give to young moms and women, this is the most important. In this day and age, accountability seems like a fourteen-letter cuss word, because so many do not want anyone helping guide, correct, or especially rebuke them. Girl, accountability was the best thing that ever happened to me. I needed someone to help me see the unhealthy areas in my life that I was blinded to and the ones I had become comfortable and familiar with. I call those areas "blindspots." You know that area of your car you can't see without assistance from a mirror, camera, or (now) alarm? We need help to see our blindspots in life.

Pastor Diana and her husband Pastor Tom (introduced in the acknowledgements) were life-changing pastors and mentors in my and my husband's lives. They have two grown and amazing daughters who love God fiercely and both honor and adore their parents. They also have grandchildren who love and serve God and cherish their grandparents. Pastors Tom and Diana have a legacy of hundreds (if not thousands) of other people who love and respect them; they have impacted so many lives. Pastors Tom and Diana always spoke the truth in love to me and to us. They also lovingly called out blindpots and familiar, unhealthy patterns that I did not or could not see. At times they held me accountable for toxic behaviors or attitudes that hindered my journey. They were always quick to share their tools, with their only motive ever being to help equip me to stay on the path that God prepared for me. I pray that you can find a matriarch to answer your questions and speak truth to you. Don't be afraid to ask someone to mentor you, and remember to always look for lasting and good fruit in the lives of your mentors. Pastors Tom and Diana drip with bushels of good fruit. *"A good tree can't produce bad fruit, and a bad tree can't produce good fruit. A tree is identified by its fruit. Figs are never gathered from thornbushes, and grapes are not picked from bramble bushes. A good person produces good things from the treasury of a good heart, and an evil person produces evil things from the treasury of an evil heart. What you say flows from what is in your heart." (Luke 6:43-45)*

You have to look for good fruit. Many people say great things on social media and post videos of their filtered lives, but that's not what I'm saying. Have you spent time with them and seen a healthy relationship with their spouse? Are their adult children still close to them, and do they still serve God? Is this someone who is emotionally and spiritually stable? About six or seven years ago, I was invited to do a book study with a group of ladies. The author of the book was a young wife and mom. The book had a catchy saying as a title and some cute stories. It became a bestseller, and she ended up with a following of millions of young moms and wives from all around the globe. Slowly her message became garbled with the world and lots of psychobabble. Two years ago, she became divorced and crashed on the curb of life, yet she had written this book teaching young women how to be moms and wives. Talking about tools is not the same as using them. You certainly don't want a

> **Talking about tools is not the same as using them.**

mentor who doesn't know how to use the tools they've been given or someone who has the same tools that you already have.

Make sure your mentor is someone who has a spiritual covering and who is personally accountable to someone else. Choose a woman who is local, not a YouTube person or an online pastor. Reading a book by a powerful woman of God does not make her your mentor. We need real women, or "Godmothers" as Lisa Bevere calls them. Pastor Diana is fifteen years older than I am. When she moved away to be with family, I was 50 years old, but I still found another mentor. This mentor is over twenty years older than I am. Choose wisely who you follow, as this will affect the trajectory of you and your whole family.

Years ago we were listening to a radio teaching or cassette tape (yes, that long ago), and the teacher said, "I'm just here to give you tools. Putting them to use is up to you." That stuck with me. I'm a visual person, so I could see myself getting tools and then using them to fix what was broken. *"But don't just listen to God's word. You must do what it says. Otherwise, you are only fooling yourselves." (James 1:22)*

Something our senior pastor says all the time is, "Be humble, hungry, and teachable." I like to also say, "STAY humble, hungry, and teachable." Those qualities are vital if you want to Momistry well. You must be humble enough to admit and repair mistakes and failures, hungry enough to work at growing in God and relationships, and teachable enough to take the tools you are given and actually apply them to your life.

One time, I was graciously thanking Pastor Diana for her wisdom and patience with me in a certain area. She said, "Patty, I gave you the tools, but you put them to use. So many people talk with me for hours and then drop the tools I've given them before they even get home." It's a choice to be accountable, and I cannot implore you enough to find a well-seasoned woman to be accountable to.

In this age, it's probably okay to just outright ask someone to be your mentor; however, in my generation the ladies before us didn't have mentors, so it had to happen organically.

> **Where there is no accountability, there will also be no responsibility.**
> —Sunday Adelaja

When you find your person, invite her to coffee or lunch, explain why you want a mentor, and then ask. Listen, if you're not willing to be accountable, receive tools, and actually apply them, don't waste her time and yours. As someone who now mentors young moms and wives, I know there is a fine line between enabling and helping. The Holy Spirit has on dozens of occasions encouraged me, firmly, to stop enabling someone. Take some time and do some self-reflection before asking.

Keep this in mind as you do your self-reflection. According to Dictionary.com, this is the definition of accountable: *"obligated to explain, justify, and take responsibility for one's actions, and to answer to someone, such as a person with more authority."*

When you do ask your person, and they say "yes," have an idea of what your expectations are. For example, if you expect to meet monthly, ask her. You might ask: "What are reasonable hours for me to text or call you?" or "Can you try to give me correction with a spoonful of sugar so I can receive it?" This method was so important for me initially, but eventually there came a time when I was frankly told, "You sound resentful, Patty. You have some real bitterness." It was the truth, I did.

Also ask, "What time frame works best for you? I'm thinking of starting with a year. Does that work for you?" Remember, they are not obligated, even if they are a pastor. If they are not in a position to mentor, then ask God to bring you someone else or do some self-reflecting as to maybe why they are not available; it may or may not have anything to do with you.

For the sake of this book, I'm focusing on seasoned mothers and/or grandmothers to mentor you in your Momistry. Mentors in school, at work, for finances, and such are imperative in life too. All of my adult children have mentors, and a couple of them have several mentors. My youngest son, who does not have children yet, likes to say, "Mom, you're the white Oprah," as I'm his relationship mentor. Please don't get offended by this statement. It is said with clean hands and a pure heart trying to honor me. If you knew my son, you would laugh, so please smile and or laugh.

Having a mentor also sets a good example for our children to receive instruction and correction. When my children were younger, I would ask them who they looked up to and how they could come alongside that person for a season and grow. For my youngest son, it was our worship pastor whom he took piano lessons from. To this day he says, "I'm not sure I learned much about music, but I sure learned a lot about character and honor." For my oldest son, it was our church's building manager, who was also the young adult pastor at the time. During a huge building project, my son would work side-by-side with this man. He learned work ethic and the importance of doing things with excellence. He also got shot in the head wearing a construction helmet with a nail gun once, and that was a life lesson all of its own.

My daughter would serve at conferences with our helps ministry leader. She learned the importance of being a servant and treating people better than ourselves. Our middle son has a handful of business mentors, and he is a well-educated, thriving entrepreneur. Our youngest daughter looks up to one of our young female pastors, who also happens to be her science teacher. When you see great Christlike character in others, know that you can have that too, if you humble yourself and ask. If you're humble and teachable (not needy), people are usually willing and happy to share tools from their toolbelts with you.

We have to be careful that we don't become needy, and we also need to listen to the Holy Spirit, pray, and read Scripture for ourselves. If a direct answer is not in the Word of God, I'd always go with wise counsel—always. If my thoughts are jumbled with my emotions and other voices, I cannot clearly hear God or discern His Word wisely. I needed someone who could be objective, not subjective. Most of the young moms or women I've mentored begin by talking with me regularly, and then it's sporadically, and then it's rarely.

**Tools only work if we use them.**

Eventually, they either no longer need my tools and are successfully using them, or they've chosen not to use my tools and have continued using the sometimes-destructive family tools they were raised with.

One young woman I mentored for a season was trying not to replicate her mom's many marriages to very unstable men. She wrote down what she wanted in a husband, attended Bible school, faithfully served at a local church, and was making quality Christian friends. Sadly, the voices of some of her unbelieving friends fed into what was most familiar to her. She quit talking with me, then stopped attending church, and now lives with a guy who is exactly the kind of person she had told me years before she "absolutely did not want." She had been given tools but didn't want to patiently do the work and wait on God.

There is always the hope of returning to the Lord, and I pray that for her. Tools only work if we use them.

Maybe the thought of having a mentor is scary or uncomfortable to you. I get it; I sure did not want or like someone coaching me or calling me out. Being rogue was the way I was raised, and it seems like that lifestyle has become more and more normal. I didn't want it, but do you know what? I sure needed it and occasionally still do. Most recently, when some dear friends left our church, I was heartbroken. My mentor came alongside me and spoke truth and wisdom to me, and she helped keep my focus on where God wanted me and my family. She had some similar stories to share and encouraging words, warm hugs, and powerful, effective prayers—some new tools for my toolbelt. Even at over fifty years old, I sometimes still need someone to help me see the truth through all of my feelings. Hopefully in my seventies I won't still be calling her, but I know she wouldn't mind at all if I did.

Be careful not to overwhelm your mentor. One time Pastor Diana told me, "Patty, why don't you type that email out and wait two or three days and then see if you need to send it to me?" As I mentioned before, I was such a reactionary person that every time something major or minor happened I would email or text her. That poor woman probably cringed when she saw my name in her inbox. I would email her not just about family stuff, husband issues, or the kids, but also when other church members and I would have conflicts, or there were conflicts between my extended family, and so on. Waiting to email, text, or call was a powertool for my toolbelt. It allowed things to spiritually and naturally settle and sometimes completely diffuse without having her holding my hand through the minor things, even if they felt major in the moment.

Fifteen years ago, a man attended our church for a season, and he had caused some very divisive issues with our family. He had been directly told by my husband and kindly encouraged by pastors to stay away from me and our family. One Sunday morning I was serving at a church service, and he walked right up to me and started talking, like we were best friends. Keep in mind this was over a decade ago, so I was still acquiring some of my tools. I'm not sure why I got so defensive; maybe because I'm a rule follower, and this man was not following the rules. I barked "You are not allowed to talk to me" in a harsh tone and stormed away.

Cue the swooning drama queen GIF. I went home and immediately emailed Pastor Diana, banging on the keys with each letter. She graciously emailed me back the next day and set up a time a few days later for us to connect in person over lunch. This woman is one of the most patient and understanding women on the entire planet. She's one in a million. She smiled and listened to my rant, though I'd calmed down quite a bit by then. She took a few more bites of her salad and said, "Patty, you know it's okay not to respond, right? When someone says something confrontational, unkind, or inappropriate, you can simply walk away. It's okay not to say anything. Unspoken words can be more powerful than spoken ones."

Mic drop! I mentioned this earlier, but this was a power tool that she gave me. Oh my word! This was such an epiphany: learning to respond and not react, or even not saying anything at all. Powertools are for specific instances and work quickly and effectively, like a drill or nail gun. Part of our Momistry is getting all of the tools we need to keep our children safe: body, soul, and spirit.

We want to have healthy relationships with our mentors. Exhausting them with our every whim is not healthy. The most difficult thing for me was simply being vulnerable with Pastor Diana. After decades of self-protection, I wanted to sugar coat things and move on. Once I finally broke down and ugly cried and let her past my walls, I started growing. That's when self-reflection was so helpful. I would talk with her but then still be carrying baggage when I left. The Holy Spirit told me, "You are only giving her access to tailored parts of your life. She cannot help you if you do not let her into those walled-off places." Yep, I heard that loud and clear.

After giving my life to Jesus, which was twenty-seven years ago, I started looking for people to help me on my journey. Mostly I found cheerleaders redirecting me to "just read my Bible," which I was struggling to comprehend being that it was KJV. I needed someone to tell me the truth: the ugly truth delivered with love. The love of Pastors Tom and Diana was such a safe place. I have heard of toxic leadership and have seen it myself, but that was not these two. Look for a loving person to be your mentor, then treat them honorably and respect their position in your life. Friendship comes years down the road. For me it was probably ten years.

When we are trying to be good wives, moms, or friends, we must find and use the correct tools needed to do those things. One quick example: I was talking with my aunt the other day via text. She's in her seventies and lives on the other side of the continent. I was going through pictures that my mom had. Mom graduated to heaven several years ago, and I didn't recognize some of the faces, so I texted the photos to my aunt to ask her. They were pictures of friends my mom had. She would have friends for a while, then they would have a disagreement, and mom would cut them off. She didn't have the tools to handle conflict or reconcile a relationship, which is probably why she was married three times as well. My aunt couldn't remember most of the people in the photos; some of them went as quickly as they came into my mom's life. Imagine the relationships my mother would've had if she had a mentor who could've helped her find and use tools she didn't have. A mentor can help you acquire tools that you don't have in your toolbelt. What if all we had was a wrench? That would be helpful if life only dealt us bolts, but life is full of nails, screws, wire, rough edges, and so on. A mentor helps you see the problem, and they can give suggestions to solve it. But ultimately solving it using the tools we are given is OUR responsibility.

Our goal should be to be Christlike in our homes first and everywhere else after that. *"Imitate God, therefore, in everything you do, because you are his dear children. Live a life filled with love, following the example of Christ. He loved us and offered himself as a sacrifice for us, a pleasing aroma to God." (Ephesians 5:1-2)* In culture today, it seems to go the other way. We put on our church face on Sundays and Wednesdays and then act like heathens at home. Joyce Meyers once said something like, "You think you have been called to have a worldwide deliverance ministry, and you haven't even taken authority over the dishes in your sink. Get your house in order before you step out into ministry." This is why Momistry is so important. Some of us have been called to do other ministry for God, but we must take a season and get our houses in order and pack our toolbelts. This isn't about a clean home. You can have a

> **The godly walk with integrity; blessed are their children who follow them.**
> **—Proverbs 20:7**

clean home that's full of strife, contention. and bitterness. It's about peace, maturity, order. and unity. God has called me to the Momistry, but He has also called me to serve, lead, write, speak, and mentor. This is one of the reasons I desperately needed a mentor—someone to lovingly tell me what was out of order, to show me when I was causing division, and to alert me when chaos was running amuck instead of peace. I needed someone who could lovingly tell me when I was being selfish or childish—one time they revealed to me I had bitterness, and another time it was offense. Speaking the truth in love kept me on the narrow path.

> **Your greatest accomplishment may not be something you do but someone you raise.** —Andy Stanley

You can find some helpful resources from successful woman/mother/grandmother leaders like Lisa Bevere from Messenger International in Colorado. She has amazing sons who love her and still serve God. Brenda Johnson, wife of Bill Johnson from Bethel Church in California, has powerhouse children that love God and their parents. One ministry that was quite impactful in our family was "Focus on the Family," with James Dobson and his wife Shirley. We used to listen to their talk show on the car radio back in the day, but I think they have a podcast now. Important note: These women and their resources cannot replace a mentor. It's still important to be accountable to someone local to you early on in your Momistry, especially before taking a platform or microphone type of position. These other ladies and ministries do have a warehouse of tools for you to utilize, but there is no accountability for you or for them. Just remember that tools only work if you use them.

When my husband and I were in our mid-thirties, we were being groomed to be church planters in a small rural area in Missouri. We had both completed degrees in Biblical Studies and had gone through the training a nondenominational group required. In our attic we literally have a huge plastic tub filled with books and training material from several different ministries. We were such hungry and new Spirit-filled disciples. We had heads full of knowledge but not much experience. Our home was not in order, our finances were a mess, and our marriage was a rollercoaster ride, but we were walking in a leadership anointing. Remember, David was anointed king over fifteen years before he was actually placed in the position of king. People could see the anointing on us and even the anointing on our children, but my character and my husband's character were not ready to lead a congregation.

Looking back, I'm certain that we would have been another statistic of quitting pastors or pastors that faltered or divorced had we continued on that path; however, we were zealous and wanted to serve God with all of our hearts, minds, and strength. We were so torn. Yet, in our spirits, we did not have peace. My husband called a pastor friend who could be more objective. He said some lovingly direct words to my husband and told us that we should be led by peace. We were not; we were being led by zeal.

We declined the position and relocated closer to a church where we could serve and be mentored, which is where we met Pastors Tom and Diana. This was a church where our children could hear biblical preaching and experience the presence of God, which are also things that are vital for your Momistry. I have a confession to make: I'm fifty-six years old and am still not ready to be a pastor. Oh, I can preach, share tools, and teach, but tolerating all of the shenanigans I pulled on my own pastors—not up to that one.

In my over twenty-five plus years of serving Jesus, I've seen too many moms sacrifice their children on the altar of ministry. These are women without mentors to encourage, equip, and warn them. They're mommas new to the faith or new to leadership without many tools in their belts. I've watched children who have stayed in my home over the years as their parents traveled and ministered. Some of the children had suffered neglect at the hands of parents with a passion for visible position and not Momistry. I call this "pursuing platforms" or "microphone mongering." I think this is probably why pastors' kids can sometimes have such bad reputations. When you've been around awhile, you hear things like "Oh, they're a PK (pastor's kid)," as if that's an excuse for misbehavior, defiance, or rebellion. That's why, when looking for a mentor/pastor, always look for the fruit in their life—good, consistent fruit. Look closely at 1 Timothy 3:1-6:

> **But those who won't care for their relatives, especially those in their own household, have denied the true faith. Such people are worse than unbelievers.**
> **—1 Timothy 5:8**

> *"If any of you aspires to be an overseer in the church; you have set your heart toward a noble ambition, for the word is true! Yet an elder needs to be one who is without blame before others.*
>
> *He should be one whose heart is for his wife alone and not another woman. He should be recognized as one who is sensible, and well-behaved, and living a disciplined life. He should be a*

*"spiritual shepherd" who has the gift of teaching, and is known for his hospitality.*

*He cannot be a drunkard, or someone who lashes out at others, or argumentative, or someone who simply craves more money, but instead, recognized by his gentleness.*

*His heart should be set on guiding his household with wisdom and dignity; bringing up his children to worship with devotion and purity. For if he's unable to properly lead his own household well, how could he properly lead God's household?*

*He should not be a new disciple who would be vulnerable to living in the clouds of conceit and fall into pride, making him easy prey for Satan. He should be respected by those who are unbelievers, having a beautiful testimony among them so that he will not fall into the traps of Satan and be disgraced."*

Read through those verses a few times. Of course, it's "he" in the Bible, because that's who could actually read back then. The vast majority of women could not, but God is speaking to His children here. Can you see the areas that you might easily overlook and where a mentor would be impactful? I can see several that I have had to overcome. Things like anger, isolation, being argumentative, and also being patient as a new or newer disciple so that I didn't "fall into traps of the enemy." Looking back, I am so grateful that we did not take that position to pastor that church in rural Missouri. It's so important to find a mentor/pastor and take the time to mature, gather tools, and become skilled at using them before sharing them with others.

Remember that being held accountable is vital to your Momistry. If you want things in your life to change, you have to change what you're doing. Here's the definition of accountable again: *"obligated to explain, justify, and take responsibility for one's actions, and to answer to someone, such as a person with more authority."* If you don't do anything else from this book, although I hope you do, find yourself a mentor. Your journey can take some unexpected turns, hit major bumps, or take completely wrong turns. Find a safe, wise, good-fruit-bearing person. The peace you will receive from a healthy covering will by far outweigh the risk.

**Momming is the best job ever and the hardest job ever. YOU CAN DO IT!**

## Prayer:

*God, thank You for the wisdom found in Your Word. Thank You for being the first One keeping me and my children safe: body, soul, and spirit. Thank You for leaders and godly examples of women and mothers following and faithfully serving You. I pray that You would bring me the right mentor or pastor to walk with me on this journey of life, someone who is filled with the Holy Spirit and one whose life is overflowing with good fruit. May the Holy Spirit give me patience and peace as I take a season to get equipped by filling my toolbelt and while I get my house and character in order. Help me, Jesus, to be and do all that God has called me to do. AMEN!*

## Practical points and questions:

1. Who in your life do you look to as a role model?
2. Is there someone in your community you could ask to mentor you?
3. What part of this chapter resonated with you?
4. What are some tools that you already have in your toolbelt?
5. How do you feel about accountability? Be honest with yourself.
6. Are there tools that you know you need to add to your toolbelt, or do you need some power tools?

# Notes:

# CHAPTER 4

# Parenting in a Sexualized Culture

> **When you teach your son, you teach your son's son.**
>
> **The Talmud**

According to the survey we took when collecting statistics for this book, "protecting children from a sexualized society" was the number one concern. 74.6% of mothers, mothers-to-be, and guardians listed this as their biggest concern in parenting today—thus, this will be the longest chapter in this book. Mommas have legitimate worries, and some have gripping fear of promiscuity, pornography, kidnapping, rape, transgenderism, and sex trafficking, as well as diseases, teen pregnancy, and the gamut. Though the internet, school computers, and cell phone accessibility may make these things more easily available, these are not new things. *"Nothing under the sun is truly new." (Ecclesiastes 1:9)* The Bible is full of instruction on sexual immorality, lust, orgies, and shockingly almost all perversities. It's a slippery slope trying to teach and steer our children away from these things while enabling them to hold a healthy, clear, biblical view of sexual relations within the covenant of marriage. Intimacy and pleasure with your spouse are beautiful benefits that God created for marriage. *"When you teach your son, you teach your son's son." - The Talmud* We have to be very careful not to get super religious, shameful, or legalistic about it.

While talking about this chapter with my eldest son, who is now thirty-four, we discussed the origin of sin and the sinfulness of objectifying humans who "God made in His image" (see Genesis 1:26). My son had some great insight into how common objectification is. When we look at someone as "hot" or "sexy," are we looking at them through a "made-in-the-image-of-God" filter? Probably not. When we see a drug addict passed out on the street in a puddle of their urine, do we see someone who is made in the image of God, or do we look with disgust and disdain? As Christians we need to be culture changers and start viewing humanity the way God created it.

This book is not a theological study; it's more of a practical sharing of experiences. Sometimes it helps me when I have a basic understanding of why. Here is my personal perspective of when sexualization and objectification started. *"Then God looked over all he had made, and he saw that it was very good!" (Genesis 1:31)* That included humanity. We humans no longer live as God created us: naked in the garden of Eden. We got kicked out (see Genesis 3:23). When the fruit was eaten from *"the tree of the knowledge of good and evil" (Genesis 2:16)*, shame came on the scene (see Genesis 3:7). Since the fall of mankind, sin and the objectivity of humanity's sexuality entered the world. Adam and Eve weren't afraid because of their disobedience; they were afraid because they were naked (see Genesis 3:10). God did not originally design us to be fearful of our sexuality. He designed us in His image and said, "It is good." Go read about it in Genesis and see how paradise was lost. With the sacrifice of Jesus, all of that has been restored; however, the sexualized culture of today, and throughout all of history, is still swimming in sinfulness. It's our job to turn the tide and to teach and train our children to do the same.

We live in a culture inundated with sexualization: movies, commercials, billboards,

> **For this reason a man shall leave his father and his mother, and shall be joined to his wife; and they shall become one flesh. And the man and his wife were both naked and were not ashamed or embarrassed.**
> **—Genesis 2:24-25 AMP**

apps, books, TV shows, magazines, and so on. It is constantly in your face and in the face of our children. Why don't we talk more about sex in church? I think it's because it's uncomfortable. Well, hey, do you know what? Welcome to adulthood. Things get mighty uncomfortable at times. I mean, have you read the Song of Solomon? It's PG-13 rated. God's original plan is clear: *"For this reason a man shall leave his father and his mother, and shall be joined to his wife; and they shall become one flesh. And the man and his wife were both naked and were not ashamed or embarrassed." (Genesis 2:24-25 AMP)* Our children will not usually hear biblical teaching on sexuality in their youth group or at church. It is our job as the parents to teach them.

Here's an important note: If you have not received healing in this area, take some time with the Holy Spirit to pray and receive healing. We don't want to perpetuate our own struggles on our children. So many of us women have body image and shame issues. At fifty-six, while I'm now pretty free in the area of intimacy, I still don't like my husband to touch my chubby belly. I grew babies in there, and it's never been the same. He doesn't care, but I shut down. Women who were sexually abused, dabbled in pornography, or were promiscuous before marriage might struggle with a tainted heart, shadows, images, and smells that they have to take time to wash in the blood of Jesus. Also, women who were raised in religious bondage about sex and sexuality need freedom from those oppressive chains. Jesus will bring freedom. He will wash everything away. We just have to ask Him. Then every time something comes up, ask again. His mercies are new every day. Mommas, take three slow deep breaths, and ask the Holy Spirit if you need healing or freedom in this area. Then take a few days to pray, do some self-reflecting, and allow healing and freedom to flow. You will be thankful that you did, and your husband or future husband will be thankful, and your children will be thankful, too.

We didn't talk about sex at all when I was growing up. My mom made comments about it as if it was a marital duty—statements like, "Oh, it's that time of the week." My mom, stepdad, and I together watched just about every R-rated movie available in the 1980s and 90s, most of which were packed with explicit sex scenes and loaded with foul language. Even books my mom recommended and purchased for me to read were murder mysteries with graphic sexual situations in them. We didn't serve Jesus when I was growing up, so sadly, I had many other influences. It's no wonder I was sexually active at fifteen and never had anyone to talk to about it—not one person. Thanks a million, Jesus, for Your healing and deliverance.

> **As long as your identity is built around your pain you cannot become free of it.**
> **—Dr. Caroline Leaf**

A few years ago, my adult daughter and I traveled to California to see my dad. He put on a movie, and within the first ten minutes there was a fairly graphic sex scene, and I had lost count of the foul language. We were at his house, and he did not know Jesus (and does not, yet), so my daughter and I excused ourselves to go to bed. Dad outright asked if we didn't like the movie and pressed the issue, saying that it was so funny. I said, "I have no interest in watching explicit sex scenes." In the 80s I could watch those movies with my mom and her second husband without feeling uncomfortable at all; I guess I was just comfortable with or dull to it back then. Now, thirty years later, I was not going to have that trash dumped into my spirit and soul, nor into my daughter's. Even though my daughter was an adult, my Momistry was to keep her safe: body, soul, and spirit. Dad was aggravated at me about the movie but changed the channel to something more lighthearted. The Holy Spirit was grieved, and His presence is precious to me. This also spoke volumes to my adult daughter, who is now in Momistry with a son and daughter of her own.

One time, our youngest son went with a friend and an elderly couple from our church to see a movie. This couple had adopted the boys as grandsons and took them on occasional outings. Fifteen minutes into the movie, the couple stood up, grabbed the boys, and left. The vulgarity and sexual innuendos (in a PG movie!) were not acceptable to them. What a powerful statement this was to two preteen, impressionable young men. The couple took them for pizza, and they had a great talk about guarding their hearts, eyes, and ears. My son still uses this story as he helps with the youth at our church and mentors some younger boys. Be prepared to walk out of a movie, turn a movie off, or throw away a DVD. We don't ever want to appear to be endorsing sexualization at the same time we're trying to encourage abstinence. Remember that we are turning the tide on culture.

Since we did not talk much about sex when I was growing up, and the sex ed film we watched in public school in the fourth or fifth grade was all the education I had, I didn't have any tools for this. Once I was in my thirties, I certainly did not remember that school movie, and I probably slept through it anyway. As a mom of three boys (and having housed dozens of others), I can tell you this is a topic that you'd better get comfortable with. (See resources for more tools.) I have a confession: It still feels awkward talking to my children about sex, even my adult children, but now I'm less concerned about the content and more concerned about their safety and the health of their sexuality.

Having three sons, I was caught off guard by the voluminous boy issues. No one had ever taught me about them. Most of it, I thought, was just teenage boy humor in movies. Well, you know what? It's real, and they need an expert to talk to about all things boy-related. You and/or your husband should be that expert in their lives. Otherwise, they will talk to peers, and that can lead down some very dark paths. I'm not writing a book on the "how to" regarding this topic, although after three sons I feel like I could. There are some amazing books out now that you can read with them, and it starts the conversation in more of an informative way, preemptive instead of reaction-based (see resources). I will say this: It's important to start talking to them about boys having a penis and girls having a vagina at an early age. That will help your child not feel shame when talking about this part of his or her body. Remember that they are created in the image of God. Say it like it's their elbow or big toe. Make sure to tell young children (under 12) that we only talk to mommy, daddy, doctors, policemen, or counselors about these boy/girl body parts. They are beautifully made by God, and they are private.

> `I have a confession: It still feels awkward talking to my children about sex, even my adult children, but now I'm less concerned about the content and more concerned about their safety and the health of their sexuality`.

When my eldest daughter was a freshman in high school, it was her first year as a teen in public school. Prior to that, she'd been mostly homeschooled or in a private Christian school. In the ninth-grade health class, they were teaching on sexuality. One of the things that the public high school teacher had the students do was walk the school halls with the boys saying "vagina" and the girls saying "penis" until the giggling from the girls and the rude comments from the boys stopped. Surprisingly, it only took one day. As a parent I was mortified, but I never told my daughter that or said a word about it. I completely understood what the teacher was doing. We must make those words more common in our homes, as well as erection, period, masturbation, sex (or "hooking up," as they say nowadays), oral sex (I'll spare you the current slang), and so on. If you need to walk around the hallways of your house saying them out loud until you feel less awkward, then do it (make sure your children are not home, or your husband—he might think it's a proposition!).

Remember the survey we did? Having difficult conversations was number two out of the ten options we presented in the survey. "How will I navigate hard conversations?" Of the hundreds of mommas, mommas-to-be, and guardians surveyed, 73.8% listed this as a top concern. My personal best answer for you on this is: "You just have to do it." Think of it like a mammogram, dentist appointment, or pap smear. We do it to check for disease and also to keep our parts healthy. Well, on the same note, we talk to our children about anything and everything to ward off diseases: smoking, drugs, obesity, and sex (outside of marriage). Becoming that safe place and expert on sex is the best way to help facilitate these conversations. If they know you're not going to freak out, you have won half the battle.

Several years into our marriage, we set up a family code called the "knee-to-knee." It's when you sit knee-to-knee with your child, spouse, or anyone and have a real, vulnerable, *no judgment* conversation. This is something

**Young people need models not critics.**
**—Kris Vallotton**

we learned from a marriage book: to only have serious conversations when you are knee-to-knee, without any distractions. It was a tool for our toolbelt that we could use for parenting as well. We also called them "family meetings" if it involved multiple people. As the parent, you can request one, or your child/children can. This is not a time to lecture; this is a time to disciple. Share stories, ask questions, and discuss cause and effect. A good phrase to use is: "If you do this, what do you think will happen?" Most importantly, listen. My eldest son is thirty-four, and we had a knee-to-knee a few weeks back over a miscommunication. It's a power tool!

Some conversations are very awkward. As they get older, it's not just about anatomy. Keep in mind your child's age. I'm going to lay out just a few potential questions you can use to facilitate these conversations. Remember not to react. If you put *any* shame or guilt on them, it will discourage further conversations:

- Do you have any questions about sex?
- Are kids at school talking about sex?
- Did you know that mom and dad have sex?
- Do you know why your sheet/underwear were wet?
- If you have premarital sex, what do you think could happen?
- What do kids call oral sex these days?
- What is your rule book on sex?
- Do you want to save yourself for your spouse? Why?

Listen carefully, and ask open-ended questions. Let them say whatever they want or need to say. They might feel shame or guilt, but you are a safe place. NO JUDGMENT! Do much more listening than talking. Then pray, pray, pray. Pray with the child present or without, whichever they can handle.

Here are a few more practical tips when having a knee-to-knee. First off, it's important that there are no distractions. Turn off the TV and silence your phone. Send other children to watch a movie, read, or play outside. We are safe, and we are creating a safe place for them. I usually start with questions that sound like "So, what's up?" if they've initiated. After the initiator has shared the topic, repeat it back to them by saying something like, "What I hear you saying is…" So many times I thought they were saying one thing, and it was something completely different. Your child could be feeling hurt or confused or angry. Children can be very subjective, and communicating clearly through all of those emotions is tough. Our job is to remain objective.

> **Love is a safe place of shelter, for it never stops believing the best for others. Love never takes failure as defeat, for it never gives up.**
> **—1 Corinthians 13:7 TPT**

It's okay to stop and pray, too. If you, as the parent, need time to digest the topic, you can ask for a "time out." I say, "Would it be okay if I take a time out to pray and get some water, and we come back in fifteen minutes [or however long you need] and continue? I need to get my thoughts and feelings in order." Kids respect this. It's also a powerful example for them in learning to manage their souls. At the end of the conversation, always ask if there's anything else that he or she needs to say.

Dozens of times, I would have a great fifteen- or twenty-minute talk with one of my children, only to find out that they hadn't shared the real issue with me yet. They were testing my response. Sometimes children make chitchat first and drop the big stuff after the waters have been tested. Ask questions, and don't end before asking, "Is there anything else?" We try to start closing a conversation with a clarifying statement like: "We discussed that your teenage friend is struggling with drinking and that it is illegal, and we know how God feels about it, but it isn't a safety issue for you, so we will pray for them, and you can encourage them to make better choices, but other than that it's none of our business." Now, if this is a friend who has their own car or drives, I would recommend reaching out to someone like a parent, school counselor, or a pastor we have in common. Sitting through one funeral for a young person who struggled with alcohol is enough, and I've sat through three.

Parents, we need to be the experts speaking truth to our kiddos. If they know that they can approach us, and they hear it from us first, other influences lose a lot of their power.

**A smooth sea never made a skilled sailor.
—Franklin D. Roosevelt**

We have an enemy that wants to steal, kill, and destroy our children. *"The thief comes only to steal and kill and destroy; I have come that they may have life, and have it to the full." (John 10:10)* It's our job to teach them, to point them to the Giver of Life, and to protect them from the plots of the enemy. Momistry is protecting our children: body, soul, and spirit.

Mommas, it's important for your children to know what pornography is, why we don't look at it, and how it's a trap. I've listed a book in the resources to read with them when they're a bit younger. Pornography is a problem for both girls and boys. One site referenced that 93% of boys and 62% of girls are exposed to pornography before turning eighteen, with the average age for first time for boys being eleven (therecoveryvillage.com). We parents have to be vigilant with cell phones/tablets, sleepovers, social media accounts, who their friends are, who they are chatting with, all the new apps and sites, and what's in their rooms. I once heard a man say, "You don't have to sneak away with porn anymore. You have unlimited access to porn right in your pocket" (meaning cell phones). With that

> **Prayer acknowledges Who God is and invites His involvement in our lost and broken world.**
> **—Lisa Bevere**

being said, talk about it, and ask them about it. By the time they're ten years old and older, it should be something they feel comfortable talking to you or their dad about. There should be no shame or guilt; instead we should be equipping and empowering them to be safe. Remember that we are momma bears, not helicopter moms. We never want them to feel shame or guilt.

Guilt has never saved anyone; God's kindness and goodness does. Kindness leads us to repentance. *"Or do you show contempt for the riches of his kindness, forbearance and patience, not realizing that God's kindness is intended to lead you to repentance?" (Romans 2:4 NIV)* I can hear the religious voices already "to spare the rod and spoil the child." I won't argue that an occasional swat for sinful, or possibly harmful, behaviors can be useful, but talking about sexuality, not participating in worship at church, not doing chores perfectly or forgetting chores altogether, sleeping through an alarm, getting a bad grade, and struggling with anger should all be teaching and training moments. Your goal should be to be their safe place, not be all judgy and condemning. Consequences should be consistent and should be done only for training, never for punishment. Of course, there are repercussions for wrong choices, but those are enforced from a gentle, teaching, humble, and loving spirit. Remember that Momistry is keeping our children safe: body, soul, and spirit. Keep in mind gentle Jesus; He let the little children come to Him, and He told others not to cause them to stumble. *"If anyone causes one of these little ones—those who believe in me—to stumble, it would be better for them to have a large millstone hung around their neck and to be drowned in the depths of the sea." (Matthew 18:6 NIV)*

I only have thirty-four years of experience to share on Momistry. As I've said before, there were a lot of failures early on. There have been successes, failures, and so many lessons learned while trying to teach. What a quandary: Most successes were first learned by failure. Thomas Edison once said, "I have not failed. I've just found 10,000 ways that won't work." Well, I didn't find 10,000 ways, but sometimes it sure felt like it. Let me share a few of my personal Mom Fail moments.

Mom Fail #1: Allowing my fifteen-year-old son to search cheat codes for an Xbox game unsupervised on my laptop was a very bad idea. He came into my room late one night carrying my laptop. He was so upset and frantic. His gaming avatar had been stuck in some video game dimension, and he couldn't get out. When he googled the cheat code, an advertisement with a barely-clothed woman popped up, targeting the demographic of teenage boys (which is evil). Although he knew in his spirit that he shouldn't, he clicked it. Of course it took him to a porn site, and he freaked out, logged out of everything, and went and called his older brother who told him, "Go right now and tell Mom." My husband was deployed with the military somewhere, so I was the default parent. He confessed, we looked at the computer's history, which confirmed his story, then we prayed and talked about the trap of pornography and the darkness it opens up with lust, perversion, and deception. Also, those images don't leave your mind; you can't unsee things. The next time we Skyped with his dad, they talked about it too. After that happened, I purchased every pop up blocker and parental control I could find, but there weren't many back then.

Mom Fail #2: A new boy at our church had invited one of our sons over to his house for a sleepover. His parents were just acquaintances to us, but they were pretty close friends with some leaders at our church. The boy didn't seem to have much of a God connection yet, so I thought my son could be a good influence on him, as they were the same age and in the same grade in elementary school. With that being said, we allowed it, regretfully. A few years later, in a pre-teen meeting at church, they separated the boys and the girls and talked about pornography. When our son came home, he told me the story of how, when he had gone to that sleepover, after the boy's parents went to bed, they got on the computer, and this other boy showed my son porn.

> **And now a word to you parents. Don't keep on scolding and nagging your children, making them angry and resentful. Rather, bring them up with the loving discipline the Lord himself approves, with suggestions and godly advice.**
> **—Ephesians 6:4 TLB**

The pastor leading the preteen meeting prayed for him, and I prayed for him too. I may or may not have gone a bit momma bear on closing doorways and pleading the blood of Jesus and restoring innocence and so on while praying. One of our pastors has said this a time or two (paraphrased): "Don't send your lambs to the mission field alone. Jesus already paid full price for the salvation of other people; your children don't need to."

Mom Fail #3: This is a two-for-one. While stationed in Hawaii, the Navy did not have immediate housing available for us, so we were put in temporary housing, which was a hotel on Waikiki beach. It sounds fancy and super cool, but six people in a hotel room for weeks got old. Well, after two weeks it got old. We didn't have access to a kitchen, so we had to eat out often. One night, as we were heading to dinner, when we got off of the elevator, we saw that the ballroom across the foyer was having a beauty contest. There were dozens of tall, scantily clad contestants roaming about. I grabbed the arm of our teenage son and was trying to steer him toward the exit doors when we noticed that the sign said in small letters "Drag Queen" under the large words "Beauty Contest." Yes, I gasped out loud and immediately reacted in my momma bear mode, shoving my oblivious teenager out the door. I then had a meltdown on the walkway. Weeks in a hotel room with children can make you edgy, even in paradise. As I ranted and raved about the depravity, I incited tons of questions from our teenage son and two of his younger siblings. Had I graciously smiled and walked my family out the door and redirected their eyes to artwork or a planter or a fish tank, it would have been so much easier. Here's Mom Fail #3B: At the time we were living on Waikiki Beach, women barely wore bikinis. Thongs were just becoming popular, and men over sixty seemed to always choose the men's brief swimsuits, too. It was like the world capital of objectifying humans. This is where we really learned about the concept called "bouncing the eyes." Bouncing the eyes is when your first glance might be objectifying a person or thing, so you look away. Sometimes, like on a beach, it's necessary to look up, look down, stare at the tree or even to sit down and close your eyes. Yep! Dozens and dozens of times, we redirected our eyes and had talks about bouncing our eyes. We discussed plain old objectifying, lust, and traps of the enemy frequently during those weeks.

Mom Fail #4: Early on I was religiously parenting and not parenting from a place of kindness and peace. As mothers, we are caregivers, guides, and trainers for our children, not tyrants or taskmasters. As a born and bred rule follower, I made *a lot* of mistakes in this area. I love the way the TLB translates this verse: *"And now a word to you parents. Don't keep on scolding and nagging your children, making them angry and resentful. Rather, bring them up with the loving discipline the Lord himself approves, with suggestions and godly advice." (Ephesians 6:4)* We cannot control our children; we can only train and teach them.

I could write a book on mom failures, and I guess that's what this book is: tools to help you *not* fail like I did. Before having a mentor, for me there was a lot of learning the hard way. The biggest lesson I learned was about reacting to the situation instead of responding with the Holy Spirit. It's good to roleplay situations with your spouse or a friend, so if and when something happens, you can respond from a place of peace with the Holy Spirit, rather than reacting emotionally.

I want to reiterate that it is imperative to be a safe place for your child or children. If we are reacting and being unstable emotionally or religiously, then our children will not feel safe bringing difficult life questions to us. These are sensitive topics, so be extra sensitive to the leading of the Holy Spirit. We should be slow to speak and quick to listen (see James 1:19 AMP). God really did a deep work in me about responding and not reacting. I do not have it perfected yet, but learning to respond has made our home a safe place for our children and many others. God also did a deep work in me on healing from sexual abuse and promiscuity. Work closely together with our Helper, the Holy Spirit. Get out your shovel and dig deep, mommas.

> **Understand this, my beloved brothers and sisters. Let everyone be quick to hear [be a careful, thoughtful listener], slow to speak [a speaker of carefully chosen words and], slow to anger [patient, reflective, forgiving]...**
> **—James 1:19 AMP**

Here are a few of the basic issues we walked (or stumbled) through over the years while raising our children in a sexualized culture. Remember that our Momistry is to keep our children safe: body, soul, and spirit. Some of these lessons we learned the hard way through failure, and others were tools given to us by others:

- It's okay to say "no" to sleepovers.
- Cell phones/tablets/laptops are privileges, not obligations—even electronics provided by a school.
- Bounce the eyes. This is huge for boys, as it keeps lust from getting a hook in them.
- Keep your heart whole for your future spouse.
- Invest in cyber security for all of your electronics.
- Safety first, without much regard to embarrassment or attitudes.
- Teach and talk about healthy sex within marriage.
- God picks gender, which is proven in a person's DNA through science.

- Modesty is for your daughter's benefit; it's *not* so she doesn't cause someone else to stumble.
- We need the Holy Spirit.

<u>It's okay to say "no" to sleepovers</u>. I shared a mom fail story already on this topic, but I could've added several more. Our job in Momistry is to keep our children safe, so after several failures, most sleepovers started happening at our house. Although there was one time—and this may have been the last time that our youngest son went to spend the night at a friend's house. There were going to be several other boys there. He was maybe thirteen, and the other boys were fourteen, but they all had known each other for years. This was my youngest son, so with him we had a safe word; in our house, "safe words" were code words our children could say or text, and no matter what we will go and pick them up, no questions asked. Our word was "headache." Decide on a word with your children to help them get out of situations that they are uncomfortable in. Also, I try not to ask over the phone what's causing the uncomfortableness; that's for the ride home. You can tell them that they have to come home to finish a chore or that dad wants them home that night or just let them play the headache card or whatever is necessary, and then immediately go get them. This word is also helpful if they are having a personal crisis and need immediate help sorting it out. Our twelve-year-old daughter uses the word "avocado." In addition to having a safe word, my kids know they can always say "My mom says I can't" and blame their exit on me.

Anyway, back to the sleepover with my son. The older boys had rented an R-rated movie from Redbox. Back in the day you could rent a DVD from a vending machine without confirming age. My son called and mentioned the movie and asked if he could watch it. I asked if he was getting a headache, and he said "yes." He already knew he wasn't to watch anything above PG without parental consent. As a reminder, my job is to keep him safe: body, soul, and spirit. It was 11:00 pm, and I dropped everything and went and got him in my pajama pants and an old t-shirt. Yep, I took him for ice cream on our way home. I was so proud of him. He took a lot of grief from his friends over the next few days at school. He was shunned and couldn't sit with them at lunch.

Quick note: A few months later, that same group of boys and a few younger ones came to *our house* for a sleepover. During breakfast in our lanai the next morning, one of the boys said, "Mrs. Noel, that movie that we rented when Sam came over sucked. He didn't miss anything." It was a good teaching moment for the almost dozen boys. I replied gently and lovingly, "Once images go into your eyes, they get stuck in your brain and can muddy up your soul and your heart, making it difficult to make good kingdom choices." It was silent for a few minutes as they all processed, and one of them said, "Yeah, that movie was a stupid choice." The movie was loaded with sex scenes and nudity, as well as violence and foul language. After that, all sleepovers happened at my house and featured occasional walkthroughs by an adult. We repeatedly toured rooms filled with smelly teenagers eating pizza rolls and drinking Mountain Dew and having sock fights—which is when boys ball up their socks and throw them at each other (yes, gross, smelly teenage boy socks). I sure miss those days.

<u>Cell phones/tablets/computers are privileges, not obligations-even electronics provided by a school</u>. Oh my, there are so many stories of taking a cell phone or tablet away, and once a computer. Listen, there is no reason for a child who is not driving to have a cell phone, in my

opinion. There simply isn't the maturity there to handle that much responsibility. If you think it is necessary, there are phones without internet capabilities (yes, they still make those). Our sexualized culture is plagued with kidnappings and rapes and unhealthy relationships that come from predators meeting children online. You don't have to do much research to find those statistics. It can happen to our children, boys and girls alike. Reminder: Your Momistry is to keep your children safe: body, soul, and spirit.

When teens are driving or riding in vehicles with friends, there are plenty of phone plans where you can limit phone numbers, minutes, and texts. There's definitely no reason for a child/tween/teen to have a cell phone or tablet in their bedroom at night—ever. If they need an alarm clock, go buy them one at Target. I just checked Amazon Prime, and you can get one for $5. Get one for them and one for you, if needed. Alright, parents, this is where we set the example and plug our own phones in on the kitchen counter at night. Some phones have programming where you can shut the data off at a certain time, too.

Keep in mind that sexting is a thing. Over the years I've had dozens of moms call me shocked and in tears when they found the sexual pictures that their child had sent or received on his or her device. Most of the social media apps have a messenger option. When my youngest daughter was ten, we downloaded a popular educational app for her on my tablet.

> **We are to be people changing the sexualized culture, not following it.**

When I went in to check her progress, there weren't any scores. When I asked her about it, she said, "I just hang out in the store and talk with the other players." This is child number five, so I knew how to find the threads. They were super goofy and silly ten-year-old girl comments, but the fact that she had the ability to chat was pointless, and I couldn't turn it off or limit it. That was enough cause for me to eat the $50-a-year fee, cancel it, and remove the app from all devices. She and I had a good talk about the possibly unsafe people on the other end of cyberland. This was a game for elementary kids to enhance math and reading, and there was absolutely no need for a chat option.

<u>Bounce the eyes. This is huge for boys.</u> One of our pastors said something years ago about having to bounce his eyes when driving through some places with risqué billboards. I immediately grabbed that tool for my toolbelt and used it with my sons and several other people who have lived with us as well. *"But I say, anyone who even looks at a woman with lust has already committed adultery with her in his heart." (Matthew 5:28)* Listen, I realize that this is an issue for girls too, but remember that my daughter had three brothers and two dads (her dad and her stepdad). She was never looking for any kind of male attention. Sheesh, I actually had to teach her how to flirt when she was in her early twenties and wanted to start considering marriage. She had never really been interested before that. There are several Proverbs about the adulterous woman and seduction and the trap of sexual immorality that can lead to destruction: Proverbs 2:16-19, all of Proverbs 5, and all of Proverbs 7. You can Google more if you want. There's also the verse about the eyes being a lamp for the body: *"Your eye is like a lamp that provides light for your body. When your eye is healthy, your whole body is filled with light. But when your eye is unhealthy, your whole body is filled with darkness. And if the light you think you have is actually darkness, how deep that darkness is!" (Matthew 6:22-23)* Training our children to be honorable with what their eyes see is so important. You have to be

preemptive and talk to your children. Train them and teach them when they're young. I sure wish I'd warned my son about pop-up ads that might appear while searching video game codes.

One time our whole family was walking around The Plaza in Kansas City. It's a beautiful open-air shopping area with restaurants, coffee, and ice cream. People come from all over the world to spend time in that part of Kansas City. Anyway, we were walking along and started to pass a certain familiar store selling women's underwear. My then twelve- or thirteen-year-old son immediately blocked his eyes from the provocative images of women in the front display windows. He said, "Bounce the eyes, bounce the eyes. That's the spirit of the world." Another time, the same son was with me, and we stopped at another outside shopping center, as I had to run into that same store. I must confess that I love their bras. They're the best fit and support I've found so far. He was fifteen or sixteen at that time, and he said he would wait outside on the bench (phew). I grabbed what I needed and came out, and he had unbolted and moved the bench so it would face away from the store. He said, "No one should have to sit and look at those women like that." The window had large posters of women seductively posed in their undergarments, and I hadn't even noticed. Also, I didn't make him put the bench back, as he had made a very valid point. Our now twelve-year-old daughter hides her face even when married people in a movie are "kissing too long." But do you know what? She has seen my husband cover his eyes or look away when there's a provocative commercial or a woman in a bathing suit. We do it out of honor and respect. These are humans made in the image of God. Remember when Noah's sons covered him in his nakedness? *"But Shem and Japheth took a garment and laid it across their shoulders; then they walked in backward and covered their father's naked body. Their faces were turned the other way so that they would not see their father naked." (Genesis 9:23 NIV)* It's that kind of honor. We are to be changing the sexualized culture, not following it.

<u>Keep your heart whole for your future spouse</u>. Now this tool came from a book that Lisa Bevere wrote called *Kissed the Girls and Made Them Cry*. Mrs. Bevere had come to a conference at our church, and I purchased the book to read with my oldest daughter who was twelve at the time. After a certain chapter, the book is adult-only reading, but we read the appropriate chapters together and talked about it. The book talks about having a whole heart to give to your spouse when you get married. This is another great tool I grabbed for my toolbelt. It's not just about virginity and sexual immorality; it's also about loving with a whole heart without pieces handed out frivolously. Each time you fall in love with someone, you give them a piece of your heart, the book taught.

As someone who had a very promiscuous life before Jesus, I knew this to be 100% accurate. We wanted our kids chasing God and their dreams, not a spouse. God would (and did) bring them each a spouse, and coaching them to wait for the right one was vital. The pressure to have a boyfriend or girlfriend is huge, starting as young as elementary school. I once had a young lady ask me if she could go on a date with one of my sons. She, too, was feeling enormous pressure from their peer group. Of course, my answer was that it was totally up to him, knowing that he was determined to keep his heart whole until he was ready to marry. Maybe this is why my adult children are so loyal to their spouses and have such wonderful relationships: They didn't go into marriages with a bunch of baggage and scars on their hearts. They had whole hearts for their spouses.

It's important to start talking about keeping their hearts whole when they're younger. I've also found that it's not wise to allow other parents to say things like "Maybe our kids will get married" when the children are in kindergarten. Seriously, no one should even be thinking about that at five or six years old. It's not even cute, in my opinion. If you speak marriage over them while telling them that sex is for marriage, and they're thinking that they're getting married to this other child one day, it can get really messy. I didn't even say those things when my children were teens, although I did think to myself a few times that this girl or that boy might be good for my son or daughter. God did *not* need my help picking out their spouses. He did an exceptionally perfect job without me meddling. (Well, other than teaching my oldest daughter to flirt and not to treat all guys like her brothers.) Encourage your kiddos to keep their hearts whole for their future spouses. Their spouses will thank you too.

<u>Invest in cyber security for all of your electronics.</u> This is the year 2022, and there are so many options. If you're reading this after 2022, I hope there are more options and/or an already cleaned-up cyberland. I'm not sure if the world is more perverse now than it has been in the past; I think, and this is my opinion, that information and people are just a click away, so it seems like it. Twenty years ago, the internet was simply a tool to connect mainframes, and we had slow-moving dialup service where you had to put the receiver of your landline telephone in a piece of technology hooked to your computer so the two computers could talk. Now, well, your cell phone is more technologically advanced than the computers used to power the spacecraft that first landed on the moon. We can Zoom or Facetime or Facebook video chat with someone on the other side of the world or several people at a time. Our computers

now talk without a phoneline through supersonic fiber networks. Can you tell I am *not* a computer guru? My millennial computer genius sons roll their eyes and, respectfully, laugh at me quite often.

Remember that our Momistry is to keep our children safe: body, soul, and spirit. I will list some resources in the index on this topic. Choose something that allows you the ability to see who they are talking to. If it's their best friend for ten years, you probably don't need to read all of the dialogue, but someone they just met at school or at a church camp or at a concert is not a safe person. There is something called grooming that goes on, and it's devious and deceptive and charmingly manipulative. If you start talking about keeping your children safe when they are young, then this won't be such an issue when they're tweens and teens. Also, I did not chit-chat with them about their private conversations *unless it* was a safety issue. On one of those radio talk shows I mentioned early on, the experts talked about the importance of trust—parents trusting their children *and* children trusting their parents. He talked about when you lose trust, you also lose freedoms, which was another tool for my toolbelt. "I'm sorry I can't trust you to have your phone back after you downloaded an app that was not safe. Remember what my job is. What's my job?" Hopefully by then they can repeat it back to you. If not, remind them: "My job is to keep you safe: body, soul, and spirit."

Just this week I had to tell a certain tween girl that her computer would need to be charging in my room, as she had snuck upstairs and gotten onto her computer without permission while the parents were downstairs watching the Chiefs winning another football game. She had gone upstairs to "get some water." Later that night, after she went to bed, the Holy Spirit nudged me to check her computer. She sure lost some trust points, which was so sad.

This by far has been the biggest concern of parents that reach out to me, which is understandable. The FBI has a plethora of information and ever-changing statistics on the kidnapping, rape, sexual exploitation, and murder of children who met someone online. I say this *not* to cause fear but to cause awareness. We are to be innocent as doves and as shrewd as serpents: *"I am sending you out like sheep among wolves. Therefore be as shrewd as snakes and as innocent as doves." (Matthew 10:16 NIV)* We are to pray and ask God for protection for our children. As their parents, God has made us to be part of that protection. Just last week, a fifteen-year-old girl in my quaint, little suburb ran away and was missing for four days, with some (adult) guy she met online. The first thing that guy did was drop her cell phone in a gas station trash can. The girl finally talked with a friend and ended up back with her family. We were all praying fiercely for her protection. God only knows what went on for those four days with her and a bunch of older teenagers and young adults. Thank God for bringing her home. The battle is fierce, momma bears!

Safety first, without much regard to embarrassment or attitudes. There will be times that you have to tell a creepy cousin, uncle, or family friend not to sit next to your child. I cannot emphasize enough that this is for sons *and* daughters. It's no longer "stranger danger"; it is now simply "people danger." Depending on the source, it is said statistically that 93-95% of molestation is by someone known to the family or a relative. In my personal experience, it was my babysitter's husband when I was in kindergarten and then my mom's second husband's two younger brothers when I was a tween and teen. I didn't tell anyone until I was thirty years old and having a breakdown; subsequently, I met Jesus shortly after. Anyway, sometimes you have to say "no" to people who want your child to go to their house without you, sit on their lap, sit next to them, camp with another family for a weekend, or whatever. Sometimes this includes free babysitting. It's okay to say "no." We never forced our kids to hug or kiss anyone. It may feel awkward that you might, or probably will, hurt their feelings, but in the big picture, what's most important?

**It's no longer "stranger danger"; it is now simply "people danger."**

On a related note: It's awkward and embarrassing when your child is acting inappropriately in a church service with some friends and you have to go, during the sermon, and get them. I've had to do this on a few occasions with a couple of my children. It's embarrassing to you and to them, but it's vital to their spiritual health to develop hearts of honor. Follow this up with, "Were you honoring God when you were doing that? Were you being honorable to the person preaching or teaching or leading us in worship?" When de-escalating or troubleshooting a situation, consider if it is something unsafe, dishonorable, disrespectful, or sinful. Be careful not to make mountains out of molehills. Remember that your Momistry is keeping your kiddos safe: body, soul, and spirit. One thing our pastor says is, "Will this matter in eternity?" That was another tool I slid into the old toolbelt. It's a great filter on handling (or not handling) situations and circumstances.

Once at a family event, I took one of my daughters for a walk after an elderly male family member kept wanting her to sit by him. He kept talking to her and would touch her. It was more awkward than inappropriate. She was old enough to be empowered to say "no" and also to walk away, so I gave her some tools and explained that overly friendly men need firmer boundaries. We went back inside, and she did well avoiding him. A couple of hours later, she came and sat next to me, and he was sitting opposite of me. He invited her to sit by him, and she said she wanted to sit by her mom. He kept pressing and even added a guilt trip to manipulate. I then firmly looked at him and said, "She is sitting with me right now, and that is where her mother wants her to be." You could've heard a pin drop for about ten seconds (that felt like ten minutes). Another relative then spoke up and redirected the conversation. That male relative was never overly friendly with her again, and still isn't, years later.

There is one rule that we tried to stick to while raising our children: We didn't ever want to have discussions, debates, or arguments with our children in front of others. We would step outside at restaurants, go to the car, or go for a walk at family gatherings; I even stepped into a cleaning closet at church with a child once. Our kiddos also knew that how they responded to correction or redirection would play a huge role in how things went for them, and it was their choice. They could manage their emotions and responses much better without an audience. When your children have embraced that your role is to keep them safe and to train them, they are a lot more likely to comply with your protection than to rebel against your training. Momistry is a hard job sometimes.

<u>Teach and talk about healthy sex within marriage</u>. One night when my oldest daughter was fifteen, she had a friend over for the night. My husband and I went on a date, and the girls were going to watch a pre-approved movie on our bed while our youngest son played video games

on the family TV. She had earned a lot of trust with us over the years. While they were lying on our bed, my daughter's friend asked her, "Does it bother you to be on the bed where your parents have sex?" To which my daughter abruptly responded, "My parents don't have sex anymore. They already have four children." The two went back and forth about it, and her friend just dropped it. In the morning, my daughter told me of their conversation, and I was mortified. First of all, you don't want your daughter and her friends talking about your sex life, and secondly, the fact that they were just so casual about it *while* laying on my bed was appalling. It was at that moment that I realized I'd taught my daughter about keeping her heart whole. I'd also taught her the fundamentals of sex, in addition to what the public school system had taught her; however, I had not taught her about the marital bed and the beauty of lovemaking with your spouse.

The next morning, we had that talk over coffee. At the end of our conversation, she said with quite an awkward tone, "Mom, I will never be able to lay on your bed again." I smiled and said, "Well, sweetie, you probably don't want to sit on the couch either, or the high-back chair, and only make food on the smaller kitchen counter." She gasped with an appalled face and all the teen drama you can possibly imagine and ran out of the room. When she returned, it was a good segue into a casual, but still extremely awkward, conversation about freedom and intimacy with your spouse and how spontaneity and creativity can be fun. Keep in mind that this was a fifteen-year-old, not a ten-year-old.

> **That day we had a life-changing talk about the holiness of the marital bed and how God created it for us for when we're married.**

That day we had a life-changing talk about the holiness of the marital bed and how God created it for us for when we're married.

Kids talk about sex at a much younger age and with a lot more openness now than they did years ago. Make sure you are the expert on sex for your child. You want them to have a happy, healthy, marital sex life when they are adults, which means keeping themselves set apart for their future spouses, whom they give their *whole* heart to, because the marriage bed is beautiful. This is powerful, and it empowers them to make the choice to abstain. It's important for them to choose for themselves and their future spouses and not be in bondage to religious rules. God gave us free will, and if you try to control your teenagers with religion, it will likely cause rebellion. These are awkward conversations, but have them anyway. Let the Holy Spirit guide you through them. God is not bothered by us training our children about things, and as a matter of fact, He instructs us to train them. *"Train up a child in the way he should go, And when he is old he will not depart from it." (Proverbs 22:6 NKJV)*

<u>God picks gender, which is proven in a person's DNA through science.</u> There is really no such thing as gender confusion. God puts gender in our DNA when we are in the womb. He knits us together there. *"For you created my inmost being; you knit me together in my mother's womb." (Psalms 139:13 NIV)* There is an enemy who likes to twist perversely God's beautiful creation. He is a thief and wants to kill, steal, and destroy. *"The thief comes only to steal and kill and destroy; I have come that they may have life, and have it to the full." (John 10:10 NIV)* Since our job in the Momistry is to keep our children safe: body, soul, and spirit, we must talk to our children about this fairly early on. I think that the reason teenagers start to struggle is because the thoughts and torment

started years before, and instead of identifying the sources of confusion and chaos with a parent or spiritual mentor, they feel shame and just try to wrestle through it on their own. If they are not equipped with the truth to fight the battle, there can be casualties. It's our job as parents and mentors to keep them safe and not leave them fighting these things on their own.

It's the same, in my opinion, with lesbianism, homosexuality, polygamy, or bisexuality. The truth brings order to the chaos. Without any hint of judgment, we must teach our children their identity and how they should respond in love to others who may be struggling in this area. God's word is full of examples on this. I tried to stick with this approach: "Did God say He knit us together in our mother's womb?" The child answers, "Yes." "Do you think the Creator of the cosmos was confused when knitting us in the womb?" The child answers, "No." "Did God make you in His image?" Child says, "Yes." "Do you think He, Jesus, or the Holy Spirit are having gender issues?" Child says, "No." Then I tell them, "You've already answered your own question. God made males with a penis and girls with a vagina, and anything else is not from God." We are always responding in love, led by the Holy Spirit, not reacting from religion or fear.

> **The enemy will always try to change God's periods into question marks.**
> **—Havilah Cunnington**

When they're a little older, there may be discussion about the verse on there not being male or female in God's kingdom. From that I just go with the fact that it's not gender neutrality; it's spiritual neutrality that Scripture is talking about. *"For you are all children of God through faith in Christ Jesus. And all who have been united with Christ in baptism have put on Christ, like putting on new clothes. There is no longer Jew or Gentile, slave or free, male and female. For you are all one in Christ Jesus." (Galatians 3:26-28)*

We have to be cautious but not condemning. Love God, and love people, all people. They are all made in His image. Your kids *will* pick up on your judgmental response or shameful comments. They might go to school with students, work with people, or even have some friends who are struggling in this area. We want to bring love and light. Regardless of what standard the sexualized culture is trying to set, remember that we are culture changers turning the tide. We must be so kind and loving to people struggling in this area. Shame, guilt, or condemnation will not help.

> **The second we start drawing lines around which people are supposed to be approached and which aren't, we've already completely missed the heart of God.**
> **—Lauren Daigle**

Our children acting self-righteous or treating someone with disdain will have the opposite effect. Remember that God's kindness leads them to repentance (see Romans 2:4). Make sure you're teaching your children to be kind and to love everyone. That's what Jesus did.

Some of us have family members who are homosexual. My uncle is, and he is literally one of the kindest and most generous men you will ever meet. He is very insightful and has lifelong friendships with so many people. He and his partner have been together over forty years, longer than most heterosexual marriages I know. My uncle loves Jesus and speaks of His kingdom with great depth. It is not my place to judge him. My place is to love him, and that I do.

<u>Modesty is for your daughter's benefit; it's not so she doesn't cause someone to stumble.</u> This one can be a real battle; however, this battle

is important to choose. Too many Christian teens are posting provocative and seductive photos on social media and objectifying themselves. They then start living for the affirmation of those likes, "you're pretty" comments, fire emojis for being so hot, and so on. Too many times this has resulted in inappropriate relationships, sexting, sexual immorality, and teen pregnancy. You may think that I'm being dramatic, but when you're my age and have seen this for decades now, you have a different perspective. Oh yes, I know the argument: "Their body, their choice." This training should start when they're nine, not when they're thirteen.

Try teaching modesty as being for the same reason as holding pieces of our hearts for our spouses. You can say: "You'll want to save your body for your husband's eyes. He may not be thrilled knowing that lots of other guys have seen most of your body before." Also ask them why they want to dress that way or post those pictures. If it's just "for fun," then they are not digging deep enough. I'd outright say: "Are you looking for affirmation? This photo looks like you might want to get people to comment and like your sexuality, not your identity and personality." This needs to be a discussion and not condemnation or shaming.

Why does your daughter need that kind of affirmation? You need to ask yourself that question seriously. Make sure you tell your daughter(s) how beautiful they are and how God created them perfectly. Remind them that they are made in His image. Compliment them daily, especially when wearing casual attire, not just when they're dressed up. We didn't struggle too much with this with our oldest daughter; as I've said, she grew up with three brothers and two dads (remember, blended family), so she got plenty of male affirmation. She could also see how the guys in her life would work on bouncing their eyes and heard them make comments about the suffocating abundance of seductive imagery out there.

This is not religion, so please don't use the line "Don't be a stumbling block for other boys and men" as bondage. It might cause body image issues. Instead, remind them that it's because they are so beautiful, and they want to keep that beauty modestly covered for their husbands one day. Sexy and seduction is for your spouse, not your Instagram feed, in my opinion.

> **Modesty is because our daughters are made in the image of God. They are so beautiful, and they want to keep most of that beauty for their husband's one day.**

One son came to me one day and showed me an Instagram picture of one of the girls in his youth group. She was sixteen but dressed like she was twenty-two and going clubbing. He said, "Mom, I don't want to see her like that. We go to church together, and I've known her since we were kids. She's like a sister to me." My son struggled with seeing his friend objectifying herself and looking seductive. This is where I first heard of unfollowing someone instead of unfriending them on social media. Ugh, I regret some unfriending that I did, not realizing what on earth I was doing. (Okay, don't laugh. Remember that when my youngest was sixteen years old, I was forty-eight years old, and technology had advanced and left me way behind.)

Once our youngest son said, when he was five or six, "Why does that woman look like she wants to eat me?"—asking about a half-naked woman on the front of a magazine in a grocery store checkout aisle. I was glad he couldn't read the magazine headlines yet, wowza. For a few years after that, he would flip some of the magazines and gossip newspapers over while waiting in line at the store, at the doctor's office, or dentist's office. He was not stumbling over this; he simply and innocently just wanted to keep his filter of his friends and women in general in the context of women being created in the image of God and not, as Proverbs says, "seductive adulteresses."

> **Modesty is about finding your identity in Jesus and not needing the affirmation of men/women.**

Earlier in this chapter we talked about all of the Proverbs that reference the seductive woman and how that's a trap of the enemy. God's girls are beautiful from the inside out. *"She is clothed with strength and dignity, and she laughs without fear of the future. When she speaks, her words are wise, and she gives instructions with kindness."* (*Proverbs 31:25-26*) Honestly mommas, you have made babies. You know firsthand that there's a huge difference between seduction and lust and attraction and love. Your children will not automatically know that. Help them. Yes, have more awkward conversations.

> **Your enemy wants to strip you, make sport of you, and merchandise your body, but your heavenly Father wants to clothe you with beauty, strength, dignity and honor that will endure.**
> **—Lisa Bevere**

For your daughters, there are super cute tankinis, one piece bathing suits, little sweaters or jean jackets to wear with spaghetti strap dresses, or biking shorts or leggings to wear under dresses above the knee. Share a story of your own dress blowing up or the pleat tearing on your skirt when a carload of males drove by and how they made loud inappropriate comments ( this is my personal example). Maybe you were even sexually harassed, fondled, or raped, or have a past of immorality. This is a good time to talk about it. You could also share the stories of a friend. These are hard talks, but necessary ones. Modesty is about finding your identity in Jesus and not needing the affirmation of men/women.

<u>We *need* the Holy Spirit</u>. I don't know how people parent (or live for that matter) without the Holy Spirit. His wisdom and counsel has proven faithful so many times. The Holy Spirit will nudge you to check a phone, ask a question, or to check the history on the computer. I rarely ignored the nudges. I'd rather err on the side of being an overprotective momma bear than be a hibernating momma bear. There were so many times that He prompted me or even woke me up to help me parent. Several times the help came in the form of teaching me how to respond in situations with love and understanding and not to freak out. He prepared me for what was coming. Our children are humans. They are, as my pastor says of humans, "faulted, frail, and foolish." We have seen almost everything from our kiddos, their friends, or the thirty-plus people who have lived with us. We need the Holy Spirit to rightly handle situations—not with man's wisdom but with wisdom from above. If you are not filled with the Holy Spirit, refer back to the prayer in Chapter 1, and be filled. If you are filled with the Holy Spirit, start asking Him daily, or sometimes hourly, for help. He is our Helper. *"But when the Helper comes, whom I shall send to you from the Father, the Spirit of truth who proceeds from the Father, He will testify of Me." (John 15:26 NKJV)*

Take some time to look inwardly and outwardly. Are you or your spouse allowing lustful, perverse, or seductive things into your home?

Are there movies and shows that you watch, with or without your children, that stir up or invite darkness? How do you dress? Do you sleep with your phone? What do your children see you doing? Is it honorable, right, and admirable? *"And now, dear brothers and sisters, one final thing. Fix your thoughts on what is true, and honorable, and right, and pure, and lovely, and admirable. Think about things that are excellent and worthy of praise." (Philippians 4:8)* When we first had our eyes opened to the need to cover our children and to set an example for them, we had a bonfire. Movies, books, magazines, clothing, and anything that wasn't Philippians 4:8-compatible went into the bonfire. The bonfire may have been a bit dramatic. We could've thrown them away or donated them. Personally, we were trying to make a statement to ourselves. The statement to our children was that we were choosing to live holy and that mom and dad are still learning and make wrong choices sometimes. To the heavenlies we were making the statement that we will not allow darkness in our home. Our homes and our children belong to God and are for His use only.

> **Keep your thoughts continually fixed on all that is authentic and real, honorable and admirable, beautiful and respectful, pure and holy, merciful and kind. And fasten your thoughts on every glorious work of God, praising him always.**
> **—Philippians 4:8 TPT**

Of all the ways the enemy roams about looking for someone to devour, I think this area is the hotbed of his activity. We momma bears in the Momistry are required to be empowered and led by the Holy Spirit. We must be alert, discerning, and informed. Most importantly, we have to be a safe place for our children to come to about anything.

We must stay close by while we combat the sexualized culture by doing *whatever it takes* to keep our children safe: body, soul, and spirit.

You may need to go back and reread some of this chapter. It is sensitive, awkward, and yet vital information. Grab a highlighter and go back through. Maybe even make some post-it notes for reminders. Sometimes I make a list of things to talk to my husband about, then we jot down our decisions. This was a powertool-packed chapter. Remember that tools only work if you use them. You can raise children who love and serve God and who love their families.

## Momming is the best job ever and the hardest job ever. YOU CAN DO IT!

## Prayer:

*Father God, thank You for these children that You have entrusted me with. Protect their innocence, and give me wisdom and guidance. Help me to partner with You. Holy Spirit, please give me eyes to see and ears to hear, so I can parent well. I need You, Holy Spirit. God, I repent right now for anything that I have done to allow dark, seductive, lustful things to come into my home or heart. I plead the blood of Jesus over my home and family. In the authority of Jesus, may every hidden, dark thing be exposed to the light and love of Jesus. My children will walk in holiness and be set apart for God's use only. They will be discerning of worldly spirits and traps. They will walk in ways that are honorable, right, and pure. Help me, God, to walk that way too, and help me to set a Godly example for them on what healthy sexuality is. In the most powerful name of Jesus, Amen.*

## Practical points and questions:

1. Consistently remind your children that your job is to keep them safe: body, soul, and spirit.
2. Set up parental controls on everything you can.
3. Decide ahead of time a code word so that you can help your children out of uncomfortable or dangerous situations.
4. How do you and your spouse want to handle sleepovers?
5. Do you need to have a holy bonfire or purge?
6. Right now, tell your child how beautiful or handsome they are. Tell your husband too, while you're at it.

# Notes:

# CHAPTER 5

# Being Married
(or a Single Mom)
with Children

> **Marriage isn't just a choice. It's choosing the same person a million times.**
>
> # Danny Silk

Guess what, ladies? One day your children will move out. They'll go to college or get married or join the armed forces or whatever. Here's my point: There will come a time when it will just be you and your husband. <u>Single mommas, don't skip this chapter</u>. You may be married one day or marry again or still be dealing with an ex-spouse, the father of your children, or a baby-daddy. Regardless, there are some good truths that you can learn here too, some powerful tools for your toolbelt.

As you already know, we are a blended family, so I was a single mom for almost four years, working full time with a six-month-old and a five-year-old. That's when I met Jesus, remember. When I was single, I gave my life to Jesus, and He became my husband before He brought me a God- and family-loving spouse. When my God-given husband and I married, I had an ex-husband, and he had an ex-wife, so I've been a married, unsaved mom; single mom; single, saved mom; married, saved mom; married, saved foster mom; and married, saved mom to dozens of people who have lived in our home. Now Stuart and I have been married for over twenty-five years and love each other now more than ever before (most days).

In one of those radio shows I mentioned in the first chapter, one of the teachers said, "You have to put your marriage first, before your children." Wait—what? Seriously? Somedays I struggled to even like my spouse, while I always had this deep love for my children. God had to retrain me so much in this area—not by mandating it, but by showing me why it was important. During the first ten years of our marriage, my second husband and I did not prioritize our marriage. We neglected date nights, and the only time our kids stayed with grandparents or something was if we were going to a church conference or a military or business event. I constantly chose the children over my spouse and would get upset at him for disciplining them or correcting in a way that I thought was too firm.

In society we talk a lot about self-care. Well, our marriages need care too. We must intentionally nourish the second most important relationship we have in our lives, second only to our relationship with Jesus. Remember that the kids will eventually move out, and you do not want to wake up that day with a stranger next to you, toward whom you have built up huge walls of resentment and unforgiveness. I think that's why you see a lot of divorce from couples after the kids are grown. Husbands who don't feel respected or loved and don't want to pay exorbitant child support might hold out until the children are grown. I've seen this numerous times. Ask God now to start softening your heart toward your spouse and even towards your ex. Yes, even towards your ex! Your Momistry is to keep your children safe: body, soul, and spirit. Children being able to see a happy, healthy (not perfect) marriage is huge for their soul and spirit.

Since during the first ten years of our marriage I did not put my husband first, there was quite the strain on our relationship early on. It wasn't until our marriage fell apart and I almost divorced him that we realized we had not been nurturing this vital relationship. We had some dear friends who prayed and fought for us; they encouraged us and shared books and videos too. We also had Pastors Tom and Diana praying for and counseling us. After our reconciliation, we vowed to make our marriage a top priority. It was a bit easier with the children being older, but we scheduled sitters and had date nights and even went away as a couple for a weekend. There's an amazing book by Jimmy Evans called *The Mountaintop of Marriage*. It's a powerful tool. I've given it to dozens of couples as wedding gifts or anniversary gifts or if they were struggling with unity in their marriage. I'm not going to talk too much about it, but it changed our marriage. Go get it! Think of it as an investment. A strong marriage makes for a stronger Momistry.

I will list some helpful books in the resources. They have helped us to discover our love languages and to learn to set boundaries (there is a chapter on that coming up, too). I mentioned knee-to-knees earlier; we do that

**Children being able to see a happy, healthy (not perfect) marriage is huge for their soul and spirit.**

for marriage talks too. Sometimes I'll bring up something on the phone, and Stuart will say, "Love, that sounds like a knee-to-knee discussion. We can talk after I get home." Make sure you are staying connected intimately. Yes, I mean sexually. It is so healthy for your marriage. Mommas, if you can muster enough strength to get out of bed with the needs of your child, you can muster strength for the needs of your husband. It's been scientifically proven that it's a need for him. One game changer for me was when a girlfriend told me about coconut oil for extra moisture, which also doubles as massage oil (and hair conditioner and cooking and healthy digestion and all kinds of other things). Get yourself some. After twenty-six years of marriage, we have better lovemaking now than ever. There were seasons where it was the furthest thing from my mind. Now, I probably initiate half of the time.

Be mindful of your marriage, and talk to your spouse regularly about connection: body, soul, and spirit.

There may be times when you need to seek marriage counseling, and that's okay and actually quite normal. People just don't talk about it openly. Remember when we talked about accountability? Well, we need that in our marriages sometimes too. It can be a pastor or a therapist, as long as they're not related to you. Counseling must be objective, and family can tend to be subjective. Be strong and free to ask for counseling; it saved my marriage.

It is hard to talk about ex-spouses and baby daddies, but we need to. These men are God's sons just as much as you are His daughter. Maybe they're not serving God, are demon possessed, are philanderers, or are just plain selfish, but we are to try to see the good in them. *"Love is a safe place of shelter, for it never stops believing the best for others. Love never takes failure as defeat, for it never gives up." (1 Corinthians 13:7 TPT)* Does birth daddy love your children to the best of his ability? Does he still make time for them? Is birth daddy keeping them safe: body, soul, and spirit? Safety is key. As the mother anointed in your Momistry, pray for your children's safety spiritually. You are powerful! Oh, and pray for the salvation of your ex; that is powerful, too.

We should only speak kind and encouraging words about our spouses/former spouses/bio-parents/baby daddies around others, most importantly in front of children in our care. Children hear everything, and they may start to resent your hostility. If you need to verbally vomit, do it to God or a pastor or counselor;

> **My dear brothers and sisters, take note of this: Everyone should be quick to listen, slow to speak and slow to become angry.**
> **—James 1:19 NIV**

they can handle it. Words are powerful, so we must learn to be slow to speak.

Sometimes we, as women, can even be hostile and ugly toward our spouses, not just former spouses or babymakers. We blow up our friend's phone or social media or everyone who will listen to us, uncovering our spouse. I have literally had to call out dozens of young wives on this, as I, too, was graciously redirected by a mentor on this early on in my marriage. Maybe we think that having unforgiveness or bitterness towards our spouses or exes gives us some sort of a pass to what God says about the tongue being "like a flame of fire" (see James 3:6). Nope, it does not. We don't get a free pass on our mouths. That's our flesh and not the Kingdom of God.

God is very clear about the power of our words, and the enemy is listening closely, so he can use them as weapons against us and our children if they are within earshot. We are to be slow to speak and quick to listen. *"My dear brothers and sisters, take note of this: Everyone should be quick to listen, slow to speak and slow to become angry." (James 1:19 NIV)* This is easier said than done, I know. I can feel the tension as I'm writing. Some of us do not want to go there in this book. It is so necessary to expose it, get it out there on the table, and clean it up. You need to be healthy in your soul and spirit in your Momistry.

Did you know that divorce is in the top ten contributing trauma factors for children? I think that's probably why God hates it (Malachi 2:16 NKJV). Listen, I was divorced and recognize the guilt and shame that tries to come. You can't change the past, so put it under the blood of Jesus and LET IT GO! If you made a baby out of wedlock (sexual immorality), Jesus' blood is powerful enough to cleanse and forgive. His mercies are new everyday (see Lamentations 2:23). BE FREE! You're in the Momistry and can't have the baggage of guilt or shame around.

Forgiving men with whom we have made babies can be so hard. I do not want to discredit that. They've hurt us and sometimes our children, family, and friends. I get it. I've been there and done that and bought a few t-shirts and sweatshirts, just so I could be bitter in every season. Mommas, forgiveness is powerful and effective and mandated by Jesus. I'm adding this prayer so you can let it go and be free from any bitterness, guilt, or shame.

> Prayer for mammas who are unmarried or have baby daddies: *Jesus, I need Your help to soften my heart toward my ex. I pray that he experiences Your powerful, life-changing presence. God, I forgive him for past hurts to me and to our child(ren). I let those hurts go right now. I want to walk in your ways and bring honor to Your name, Lord. I cannot do this without You. If I have been controlled by my ex in the past, I cancel that control by the blood of Jesus. I will only be controlled by the Holy Spirit, and I will walk in forgiveness to everyone, including my ex. I release bitterness, guilt, and shame and leave them at the foot of the cross. May my hands be clean and my heart pure. Thank you, God, for new mercies every day. Amen.*

I have a confession: This was a major battle for me early on in my walk with Jesus. God and I had numerous long, hard talks about forgiving everyone and loving enemies. The first five years that my second husband and I were married, we were sued by either his ex or my ex, each time them wanting full custody of the children. It was so difficult and emotionally exhausting and a fierce spiritual battle, not to mention expensive. Not only does God hate divorce, but it's also expensive for you and your children. I made so many mistakes in this area. I complained (or verbally vomited) to way too many people about our legal battles and lost sleep and peace to the tormentors that came when I tried to rely on the ways of the world (while claiming to walk in the Kingdom). I was so defensive and not yet in a place to trust God as our Defender.

There was such a transformation in thinking and behavior that had to take place with me. I'm so thankful that I had a good mentor/pastor. As I mentioned earlier, divorce and dysfunction were rampant in my family, and I had no idea how to be married or how to be a mom. This took time to walk out, so be patient in the process and, again, apologize and repent when needed. Always move forward. Do not set up camp in a place of dysfunction.

> **Do not set up camp in a place of dysfunction.**

I remember when we first got married, my husband prayed for his ex-wife. They had gone through a horrible divorce, and the contention continued for over a decade, yet he would pray for her regularly. I would listen and agree with my words, but my heart was hard. He would also pray for my ex-husband. Our divorce was also quite hostile. My husband has this way of giving those things to God. As a momma bear, I took more of a get-out-the-way-because-I-have-my-claws-out kind of approach, but through this time of prayer, God changed my heart. My husband was praying for them, and I was the one changing. After a few years (yes, I can be a slow learner), God showed me the hearts of both of these ex-spouses and revealed how He hates divorce but can turn anything meant for evil to good. *"And we know that God causes everything to work together for the good of those who love God and are called according to his purpose for them." (Romans 8:28)*

Originally, I wasn't going to include the topic of dealing with ex-spouses and baby daddies, but apparently God really wanted me to. When you make a baby with someone, they are most likely going to be in your life forever. You see them at school events, graduations, visitation exchanges, weddings, the birth of grandbabies, deaths in the families, and other major life events. It is best to do what we can to make peace and walk in love with them. *"Do all that you can to live in peace with everyone." (Romans 12:18)* After all of the years filled with quarreling and numerous legal battles and *so* many hateful words and harsh emails, we are all now friends. We aren't best friends, but we all wish the best for each other and can have friendly conversations and greet each other with endearing hugs.

The day after my eldest son's wedding, we had a family and friends brunch in the hotel restaurant where we were all staying. The hotel had put several tables together. Everyone was talking and laughing. It was truly a heartwarming celebration. There was a buffet so people could eat and mingle. There were cousins, aunts, grandparents, family friends, and so on. I went back to the buffet for more food, and as I was walking back, I saw my ex-husband standing at the edge of

> **It is easy to love the people far away. It is not always easy to love those close to us. Bring love into your home, for this is where our love for each other must start.**
> **—Mother Teresa**

the dining area where everyone was seated. He looked perplexed and lonely, so I walked over and tried to seat him somewhere that he would feel welcomed and comfortable. I was an usher at church for over ten years, so if I ever try to seat you, it's in my blood.

Anyway, he didn't want to sit. He started smiling, and I asked him what he thought of the wedding, to which he replied, "It was great." He then asked me, "What is this?"—while waving his hand toward the table full of people. I said, "What is what?" I mean, there was a lot going on in that room. He replied, "These people. Look at our children; they're so happy. These people are so happy, and something is going on." A tear streamed down his cheek, and you could feel the presence of God gently sweep in. I put my hand tenderly on his arm and said, "This is what Jesus does: He restores, and He reconciles and makes dark things light."

He continued to smile as a few more tears flowed and said, "It's beautiful, Patty. What you did here is beautiful." I slowly responded, "This was not me. This was Jesus. He makes all things beautiful." I stood there with him for a few minutes, arm-in-arm, both of us gently crying, beaming, and savoring the moment. After a bit, someone walked up and made a joke, and we embraced quickly and went on with the day. What would that all have looked like if I hadn't let go of all the offense and hurt and chosen God's way? Be encouraged to let it go!

> **Forgiveness is an action, not a feeling.**
> **—Corrie ten Boom**

Here we go with too many stories again. This one's funny. When our middle son graduated from Stanford University with his master's degree, most of the family attended. Of course that included his mom (my husband's ex-wife) and sister. We never did yours, mine, and ours; all of the children were always ours. By this time, my husband's ex-wife and I had an amicable relationship. This was in California, which is the hub of every liberal flow you can imagine. I kept joking with our son, "Introduce us as your two moms." He did not know what to think, as he was still a little awkward when we are all together, because it used to be so contentious. He never would do it, and we missed a prime opportunity for some good California fun. Oh now, don't go getting religious on me with lesbianism being sinful or whatever. We are not lesbians, and we were joking. I feel like God is more offended by gossip and division and self-righteousness than joy and lovingly building connection. His mom and I sure had a good laugh about it.

My husband and I actually ended up taking her and her daughter to the train station so they could get to the airport in time to catch their flight home. There was not one drop of tension, and we had such a good talk in the car. I have no idea if they are believers, but they know we are. People are not going to be attracted to us being self-righteous, but the joy and love of Jesus are plenty attractive. We have been asked to pray when my husband's ex and/or her relatives have been sick or having surgery; we were, and still are, as much light as we are allowed to be. Momistry is so often discerning the situation and trying to bring love, light, and life to it. You see Jesus doing that in the Gospels, approaching each person differently. Shine bright, mommas, especially to your exes.

When you're a young bride standing at the altar getting married, you do not realize how much work it is. We are all so caught up in the moment with the dress, makeup, hair, sparkly ring, and honeymoon that our heads are in the clouds. Even in premarital counseling, you only get a peek into what struggles you might have. After bills, work, in-laws, cooking, cleaning, sex, and laundry, it's easy to be overwhelmed. You can be totally caught off guard by the way your husband leaves socks around, or you can drive him crazy with the way you squeeze the toothpaste, or maybe you like a cool room with tons of blankets, and he likes a warm room with just a sheet. Learning to compromise is huge. Sheesh, get two tubes of toothpaste or a twin size electric blanket or whatever you need to in order to quickly eliminate the easy conflicts. If

> **The greatest marriage is where two servants are in love. A servant spirit is the key to success in marriage and every important relationship.**
> **—Jimmy Evans**

you need to, get a mentor or pastor to help you with your perception of things. It's easy to be blinded to simple solutions when we are so subjective. Marriage is about serving your spouse, not about being served.

*"Sitting down, Jesus called the Twelve and said, 'Anyone who wants to be first must be the very last, and the servant of all.'" (Mark 9:35 NIV)* Oh man, no one likes to hear that. If you're not feeling the love, then be more loving. If you're not feeling romanced, then be more romantic. If you think the grass is greener on the other side of the fence, try watering and tending to the yard you're in. Remember that it's your Momistry and marriage, and sometimes that's hard work.

God has brought three of our children the perfect spouses—perfect for them. Never pick a spouse for your child. I mentioned in the last story that when our oldest son got married, it was such a marvelous day. The ceremony, the pictures, the reception—everything was marvelous. During the dances, my son and I did the traditional mother of the groom dance. He was smiling so big, and he grabbed my hand. We started moving around the dance floor, and I said, "The wedding was so beautiful. Everything was perfect. I couldn't be more proud of you." He smiled and gave his wife all the credit. I smiled back and felt the Holy

Spirit sweep over us. I said, "Son, you died today. It's no longer about you. It's all about caring for your wife. Marriage is about being a selfless servant, so serve her well, and one day you will serve your children." Through a smile that was still lighting up the whole room, he shed a few tears, as did I. I cannot even recall the song we were dancing to, but I can recall his huge smile and his heart exploding with joy, peace, and love that day.

Mommas, this is what it's all about: priceless moments like this with our children. We must serve our spouses and children selflessly, because Jesus is the Servant Savior. *"For even the Son of Man did not come expecting to be served by everyone, but to serve everyone, and to give his life as the ransom price in exchange for the salvation of many."* (Mark 10:45 TPT)

I was raised in a family where divorce was always an option. My mom's mom had been married numerous times, and my mom had married and divorced a couple of

> **Momistry is so often discerning the situation and trying to bring love, light, and life to it.**

times, and my aunts did as well. Ironically, my father never remarried after my mother left him. He is in his eighties now and lives alone. He has had several girlfriends over the years but chose not to ever remarry. There's a lot of trauma in my old family line of alcoholism, poverty, perversity, sickness, and divorce. It was a huge battle for me to break these patterns off my life. It took Jesus! Never give yourself divorce as an option, and never ever say it to your spouse. The enemy wants to destroy your marriage. Don't hand him tools to do so.

I remember a time when a friend was praying for me and said, "That destructive family pattern be broken now in the name of Jesus."

She had no idea about my family's history, as we were not that close. After she prayed, it was like my eyes were opened, and I could see how I would fight against my husband and not against things that would come to try to divide and destroy our marriage. For my marriage and family to survive, I was going to have to change the way I was doing things. That day that my friend prayed for me, I changed—not my husband.

While we were in counseling with her, one of the golden nuggets and tools for my toolbelt that Pastor Diana said to me was: "Patty, why don't you focus on the 10% that's right with your husband and not the 90% that's wrong?" Of course, there was not *that* much wrong with my spouse, but the wrong was all I focused on. It was definitely all I talked to her about. As soon as I started focusing on what was good and great about my husband, our marriage started to change. My respect level for him increased, and our connection and intimacy increased. *"So keep your thoughts continually fixed on all that is authentic and real, honorable and admirable, beautiful and respectful, pure and holy, merciful and kind. And fasten your thoughts on every glorious work of God, praising him always." (Philippians 4:8 TPT)* I've shared that nugget from my mentor with so many young mommas and women over the last fifteen years. Those wise words from her, again, changed *me* that day, not my husband.

One of the books we read when we started focusing on building a strong marriage was called *Love and Respect* by Emerson Eggerichs. In a nutshell, it was about how women need love and to feel loved and how men need to be and feel respected. It was

> **For my marriage and family to survive, I was going to have to change the way I was doing things**.

based on this Bible verse: *"So again I say, each man must love his wife as he loves himself, and the wife must respect her husband" (Ephesians 5:33)*. My generation comes from seventies and eighties sitcoms filled with sarcasm and cutting comments under the guise of humor. My family was quick to joke at someone else's expense, and my mom could be a very harsh, critical person.

As I'm remembering how hard I was on my husband during our first ten years of marriage, I realize it's a miracle that he stayed with me. Thanks a million, Jesus. Instead of being someone encouraging and uplifting to my husband, I would put him down and even berate him at times. The Methodist pastor that married us said, "Patty, you have quite the silver tongue that's quick to cut." I had only been saved less than a year when he said that. I had no idea that it was a rebuke. I mean, in my family the person with the last word or best comeback was the winner. Ugh, it makes me so sad to think back. My husband did (and does) a wonderful job of showing love to me, and I was tearing him apart with my horrible disrespect. God says, *"Guard your speech. Forsake obscenities and worthless insults; these are nonsensical words that bring disgrace and are unnecessary. Instead, let worship fill your heart and spill out in your words"* *(Ephesians 5:4 TPT)*. The book *Love and Respect* challenged and changed *me*, not my husband.

Our children and fellow Christians and even co-workers and neighbors will see our marriages through how we speak to and about our husbands. Are we telling others of their great faith, their hard work, their foot rubs, and their help with bathing the kids or taking the trash out? What are we saying about our husbands? It is so sad when we see that the divorce rate in churches is as high, and sometimes higher, than it is in the world. Our children see the dysfunction and hypocrisy and can tell when we're wearing religious masks. They see if we're acting one way at church and then another way at home. If we want our children to have good marriages, then we must set that example for them. Sometimes that means your children know that you're getting marriage counseling. Let them hear you apologize to them and to your spouse. Let them see and hear you pray together.

When our children were younger, we would sometimes have family prayer times, and they would each take a turn to pray. We weren't telling them how to pray but instead letting them learn to talk to God and see and hear us talking to God. If you haven't been doing this and you want to start, you just say to your family: "Hey guys, I was just reading this book, and this grandma lady was telling me how she used to pray with her children. Let's start praying together on Monday after dinner." Saying something like that will do just fine. When our marriage fell apart and I threw my husband out (which is so embarrassing to say), my youngest son prayed fervently for our marriage. He was nine years old. God heard the prayers of that young man, and God still hears them today. Our children are watching and learning from us.

Make your marriage a priority, mommas. Remember this: a strong marriage makes for a stronger Momistry. When you're fifty or older and the children have all moved out and it's just you and your spouse, you will be so thankful. You'll be thankful for the deep talks and dreaming together again and travel planning and, well, just sleeping with the door open or walking to the fridge in your underwear (or less). It's so freeing. We forfeited that when we adopted, but those days will be here again soon. I loved the season of being in the full time Momistry; however, this season of Grandmomistry is pretty amazing, too. Both jobs are training and keeping my children and grandchildren safe: body, soul, and spirit.

**Momming is the best job ever and the hardest job ever. YOU CAN DO IT!**

## Prayer:

*God, thank You for Your covenant of marriage. I thank You for my spouse and ask that You protect our relationship and keep him covered. I repent of any unforgiveness, bitterness, or disrespect that I have had toward my husband. Please give me the wisdom to be the wife that You've designed and called me to be. May I serve my husband and family from a place of humility and honor. God, Your ways are higher than my ways, and I embrace Your ways. Holy Spirit, help me remember to make my marriage a priority and to keep a strong connection with my husband throughout this season of parenting. Jesus, thank You for showing me what being a servant looks like. By the power of Your blood, Jesus, I break every plot to divide our marriage or our family. May every family pattern of divorce and dysfunction be cut off now, in the name of Jesus. Today I pledge to respect my husband and serve him as his helper and partner. Amen and amen!*

## Practical points and questions:

1. If you have an ex-husband or a baby daddy, forgive and let him go. Do it for yourself and your children.
2. Decide today that divorce is not an option for you (unless there is abuse or adultery involved and you cannot forgive and move forward).
3. Look for what's good about your spouse—every single little thing.
4. Plan a date night monthly or weekly.
5. Be transparent with your spouse, as vulnerability makes way for a deeper connection.
6. What are you doing well to water the grass on this side of the fence? Celebrate successes!
7. What can you start doing today to make your marriage stronger?

# Notes:

# CHAPTER 6

## "I Will Never Be Like My Mother."

## All that I am, or hope to be, I owe to my angel mother.

## Abraham Lincoln

"I will never be like my mother." Don't most of us say that at some point in our lives? Some of us have had very difficult, even traumatic, childhoods that we do not want to replicate. We can't really relate to Abraham Lincoln's quote: "All that I am, or hope to be, I owe to my angel mother." After talking to hundreds of other moms, I would say probably close to 75% of us didn't have a healthy upbringing, and half of those moms had been outright abused: emotionally, sexually, or physically. Dare I also say *religiously*? As mentioned in the previous chapters, my childhood was also traumatic. So how do we actually walk out parenting that is *not* like our mothers' and avoid passing down unhealthy generational things, like the Bible talks about? *"You must not bow down to them or worship them, for I, the Lord your God, am a jealous God who will not tolerate your affection for any other gods. <u>I lay the sins of the parents upon their children; the entire family is affected—even children in the third and fourth generations of those who reject me</u>." (Exodus 20:5, emphasis mine)*

God slowly showed me patterns from my family line that needed to be changed. It has been a journey and a fierce fight to break those familiar cycles. We all know the story of David and Goliath (1 Samuel 17). Did you know that before David killed Goliath, he killed a bear and a lion? *"But David said to Saul, 'Your servant has been keeping his father's sheep. When a lion or a bear came and carried off a sheep from the flock. I went after it, struck it and rescued the sheep from its mouth. When it turned on me, I seized it by its hair, struck it and killed it. Your servant has killed both the lion and the bear; this uncircumcised Philistine will be like one of them, because he has defied the armies of the living God. The Lord who rescued me from the paw of the lion and the paw of the bear will rescue me from the hand of this Philistine.'" (1 Samuel 17:34-37 NIV)*

Sometimes you will have a lot of smaller fights to win before stepping onto the battlefield and defeating a giant. For me it wasn't just maternal patterns that I had to battle, but also paternal. Some lions and bears I faced were alcoholism on both sides, physical abuse on both sides, perversion on both sides, emotional abuse on both sides, poverty, religion, anger, pride, selfishness, infirmity, rejection, and fear. The first step was to gradually identify each one of them. I'm thankful that God showed them to me slowly; otherwise, I may have not been able to eventually stand before my giant, which I will talk about later in this chapter.

Listen, ladies: If God and I can redirect the trajectory of my family, so can you with God's partnership. Understanding the "why" behind the battle is

> **If you didn't come from a stable family, make sure a stable family comes from you.**
> **—Dr. Caroline Leaf**

helpful. At least, it was to me. Did you know that God gives us a choice, a choice between blessing or cursing? Some of our parents, grandparents, or great-grandparents chose cursing (see Deuteronomy 30). It takes time to identify the areas where they broke agreement with or refused to obey or outright rejected God. Those things are the gateways through which the enemy has access to us.

You may hear the saying "familiar spirits" in Christian circles. These spirits are very difficult, if not impossible, to spot. Do you know why? Because they are familiar—comfortable, even. Think of those comfy shoes you wear and completely forget that you have them on your feet. They may be ugly, stained, and worn out, but you hold onto them and even still wear them because they're so cozy. It can be that way with unhealthy family patterns too. We hold onto them because they're comfortable, and we are even cozy with some.

We must listen to the Holy Spirit and listen to wise counsel. I'm so grateful for both. At times the Holy Spirit would flash an image of my mother before my eyes as I was reacting to

> **When we trust our 401K, investments, or cryptocurrency more than we trust God as our provider, then we have an idol in our lives.**

something; then He would show me the pattern in her life and also in mine. Repenting and praying in the powerful name of Jesus is the only way to break family curses or patterns and to be set free from familiar spirits. Jesus paid full price for our freedom on the cross. His blood is powerful enough to break EVERY chain.

One time, I was quite distraught about our financial situation. This was about fifteen years ago when my husband's business collapsed like a train of dominoes. We had all of our vehicles repossessed and our home foreclosed on. The failing business also took my husband's credit score down the drain. He was the major breadwinner, and we had four children at home and two school of ministry students living with us as well. Apartment buildings wouldn't even rent to us. We were forty-eight hours away from being homeless. The next day, I went to look at a townhome; I had pretty much lost all hope and didn't have another plan.

The property manager met me at the address. My oldest daughter and youngest son were with me. It was a very nice townhome, but small. The property manager had already had me fill out an application and pay the application fee. She was a lady in her early sixties, and she was very reserved and a bit snobbish in her Lexus, with her perfect hair and makeup, carrying a Louis Vuitton bag. She had our application with her, as well as our credit report. After we looked through the townhome, she and I moved to the kitchen area, and the kids sat quietly on the small hearth around the fireplace in the room next to us. She said, "Sweetie, do you know what your credit report looks like?" I nodded my head "yes" and looked her right in the eye and explained our situation. She dropped her head, and we stood there in silence for several long, awkward moments. When she finally looked up, she said, "I happen to own this property. Under any other circumstance I would not rent this or any other property to you. I don't even know how you'll get the gas in your name with this credit, but I clearly hear God telling me to give you kids a chance." I hugged her, and yes—I cried, and I still do just retelling the story.

As we pulled away from the townhome, the Holy Spirit exposed my family line of poverty and financial issues and how I had faith in the natural and not in the supernatural provision of God. He reminded me that God only wanted good for me and my family. After taking that pattern to Jesus, He broke that bear off my life. That was an intense season and an intense battle, but we won! Our family lived in that townhome for two years, and we were never late to pay our rent, not once.

God used this difficult season to show me a hereditary curse on my life. Both my mother and father had a very unhealthy perspective on money. My mother never had any and was constantly looking for the next dollar; my dad came from a family with money, but he has struggled with its grip most of his life. Money being an idol seems to be the white-collar sin of this generation. When we trust our 401K, investments, or cryptocurrency more than we trust God as our provider, then we have an idol in our lives. Like David killed the lion and the bear, this was a bear for me. God wanted to help me slay that bear. He opened my eyes to see how I was always looking for the next paycheck instead of looking to Him for provision.

> *You must not bow down to them or worship them, for I, the Lord your God, am a jealous God who will not tolerate your affection for any other gods. I lay the sins of the parents upon their children; the entire family is affected—even children in the third and fourth generations of those who reject me. <u>But I lavish unfailing love for a thousand generations on those who love me and obey my commands.</u> —Exodus 20:5-6, emphasis mine*

Alcoholism or addiction was also a family pattern. My husband is a recovered alcoholic with over thirty years of sobriety. It's been in his family for generations. Addiction is a vicious battle and is more like the lion from David's battles. Addiction is sneaky and loudly likes to pounce on its prey. Alcoholics Anonymous had a huge role to play, but only after my husband had a powerful encounter with the living God was he delivered from alcohol's grip. We have had numerous addicts and alcoholics come through our house over the last twenty years, some for healing and respite, some for detox, and some for a safe person to pray for them and take them for help. Our home is a no-judgment zone, so people can come for refuge and safety. Addicts need to surround themselves with giant slayers, not other addicts. God was faithful to slay that giant in my husband's life, and through that God was able to deliver several others from the claws of addiction too. He is faithful to save and deliver. We need God and each other for these fierce battles.

One day, I was driving home from the grocery store and saw a young man with his hood pulled up wandering around in our neighborhood. He looked disheveled and completely out of place, as we have mostly elderly neighbors. I think my husband and I may be the youngest people on our street, or close to it anyway. I pulled into my garage and didn't give it another thought. I unloaded my groceries and started putting them away. Suddenly, I hear my front door open. Please note that at that time my son was at school and my husband was deployed overseas somewhere, so I was home alone. Startled, I walked into the living room, and there stood this hooded young man. It was the son of some dear friends of ours. I'll call him Fred.

> **People don't change by being judged. People change by being loved.**
> —Craig Groeschel

Fred knew where our spare key was and let himself in, which was common for most people who have lived with us or who are close to our family. It had been awhile since we had seen him, but he still fit both categories. He was super high on meth and was delusional and paranoid. I got him to sit down and looked at the sores he'd scratched on his face and arms. Then there was a knock at the door, and it was one of the pastors from our church. Fred had borrowed someone's cell phone while out walking, and he used it and called our church. The pastor sat with Fred while I called my brother.

My brother was a recovered meth addict and giant slayer. God powerfully delivered my brother from that giant in just one night with no detox needed. Anyway, Fred was super high, dangerous, and needed to detox. He was quite stubborn, so his journey would be different from my brother's. After about an hour, I got Fred into the car to go get my brother. After Fred made several attempts to get out of the moving vehicle, I had to use my mom voice on him. He also refused to leave my house unless I let him carry a butcher knife from the kitchen, as he was certain that people were trying to get him. Listen, this was such a risky situation, where my flesh felt afraid and worried for Fred. But my spirit was at great peace as God gave me strength. Yes, I could've just called the police or an ambulance; however, I did not feel peace about those options.

After Fred and I picked up my brother, we went to the VA Hospital. Getting Fred out of the car and into the hospital took another good hour. I had to walk in front of him and my brother behind him all the way across the huge parking lot and into the emergency room. See, Fred is an army vet. He served in the Middle East and watched his battle buddies get blown up in a vehicle from an IED. He is one of my girlfriend's sons. At that time, she was on the mission field overseas. Fred had also been a close friend to my eldest son when he was growing up. Fred came back from war fighting totally different kinds of battles: a lion, a bear, and a giant.

Alcoholism also ran in Fred's family. It took him a few more relapses and a small stay in jail before he surrendered and really found God and held onto his sobriety—remember the sneaky lion. While in jail, Fred held Bible studies and led numerous inmates to the Lord. Fred is now several years sober and is happily married. He and God killed that lion and then the giant and broke that generational cycle in his family. Jesus is a giant slayer!

The struggle with giants, lions, and bears started for me when I first met Jesus, and the grip of fear was exposed. This was a lion in my life. This hideous thing had tormented and stalked me since childhood. My mom loved to laugh and tell the story of three-year-old me waking up from a dream shaking and screaming, "He's ugly, and he's right there with hair on his back." She joked about it during my teen years, too. Mom didn't know Jesus then. It was at that time that fear gripped my life. I would have horrible night terrors and couldn't sleep in the dark, even into my adult life—twenty to twenty-five years after that dream.

Several times a week, breathtaking anxiety and fear would grip me while walking to my car in the dark or opening my closet. Even trying to go to sleep was a battle every night. To some this will sound flakey, but it wasn't always just a feeling inside of me. Sometimes I could feel the cold, clamminess, or a chokehold in the physical. I remember when that lion was slain in my life. It was something that had hindered and tormented my mom and grandmother too. I'm not sure how far back it went, but this was my first family pattern battle, and Jesus dealt with that lion quickly and fiercely. All I had to do was trust Him. Do you know what? God has always taken such good care of me, ever since I gave my life to Jesus. He has only been good to me and my children.

When our oldest daughter was young and fear tried to come into her life, I was able to pray and fight off that lion. I was also able to teach her to use praise and worship and the Word of God when fear tried to creep back in. It was great to watch her teach those tools to our youngest son when he, too, battled fear that was trying to grip his life. Fear did not grip any of our children. That lion was slain, and that family curse was broken.

Family giants are a different battle than lions and bears, and they are different for everyone. They require tremendous faith and persistence until the end. It's a war that can be lengthy. For me, it was the giant of rejection. It was a generational thing on both sides of my family. I'm not sure that my dad ever felt accepted by his parents, and my mom for sure felt rejection from her father. Neither of my parents had many long-term friendships in life. Dad has one set of friends that he used to work with, but other than that it's just guys he golfs with. Mom's funeral was packed, but almost everyone in the room were members of our church, which she had begun attending a few years before her passing. There's a lot of divorce and shunning of family and friends on both sides of my family tree. There were months during which my mom did not talk to her sisters. My dad did not talk to his brother for over thirty years.

Looking back, I can't think of one healthy marriage or relationship on either side. Maybe my mom's two younger sisters had a good relationship with each other. Rejection is easy; love is hard. Rejection caused me to not allow people to get close to me, including my husband and children. This was a giant in my life, and I was going to have to walk with God to slay it if I wanted to break that pattern and have a healthy family. Please notice that I said *healthy* family, not "perfect" or "normal," as there's no such thing.

During one church service, the sermon topic was about exposing and overcoming rejection. At that time, I was familiar with that taunting giant and had learned to cave into its threats, just like the Israelites being taunted for days by Goliath before David showed up. Take a minute and go read the recount of the event in 1 Samuel 17. Certainly after the first couple of weeks, the Israelite soldiers got used to the taunting, and they were no longer shaking and terrified. By the third and fourth week, I can imagine the soldiers playing cards, laughing, and telling jokes in their tents on a hill. They'd become familiar with the threats but were still unconsciously gripped by them.

During that church service, something was said about God wanting to be with us. He created us to be with Him, and He would never reject us. I quietly gasped. Do you know that feeling when all the air in the room just leaves? That's how I felt. The Holy Spirit clearly said, "Patty, I will never leave you or forsake you. I will not reject you." I started crying in my seat. I don't remember anything else the pastor said. For the next several moments, it was just God and me and His overwhelming, unfailing love.

After the message, a prayer partner prayed with me: "Every generational curse of rejection be broken." It was like I could see colors for the first time in my life, like my eyesight went from 3D to 4D. Eh, that probably sounds flakey too, but it's the best way I can describe the transition. Perfect peace burned inside of me. The slingshot had been released, the stone struck, and the giant fell. It was so freeing and absolutely beautiful—total and absolute unconditional acceptance by God, my creator.

Wow, that's so powerful. I wish I could say it ended there, but it did not. Guess what else you have to do to a giant? It's not beautiful at all. Go read 1 Samuel 17:51, because it's really quite gruesome. You have to cut that giant's head off. Ew, that sounds gross, like something out of a horror movie! Well, friends, you have to completely cut it off. This does not mean cut off your family (unless it's someone truly abusing you, in which case setting new boundaries may be required, and we will talk about that more later in the book). It means you have to cut the giant off at the source. For me, the source was rejection, so I had to stop falling apart every time someone rejected me, especially my father.

I would literally pray out loud, sometimes loudly, before calling or Skyping with my dad. Rejection from friends, my children, or whomever: I could no longer be moved by it. Oh, people were going to still reject me, but God never would. Several nights after being free from rejection, I laid my head on my husband's chest and cried in the safety of his arms. Before that, I never really allowed him to see that side of me. We called it "a turtle." Whenever I was in a situation or with someone who might reject me, I would crawl into a shell of self-protection. Usually I'd mask it with jokes or silence. The fierce, gruesome battle was worth it, and generational enemies were broken off me and consequently off my children and their children, unto a thousand generations.

As I mentioned in the first chapter, we have had dozens of people live or stay with us over the last twenty years. One sweet girl moved in with us to attend the Bible school at our church. She was a pastor's daughter, was super funny, loved our family, and was always so helpful around the house. She even went with us on a family vacation one summer. For privacy, we will call her Lisa.

> **It ran in my family until it ran into Jesus living inside of me.**

As a pastor's daughter, although her father is now deceased, the expectations that had been put on her were overwhelming. It sounded like her dad was a real taskmaster. I didn't actually see any of it, but from what I heard, it was borderline if not actual abuse. Her father and her mother were both recovered addicts. Lisa could be really up and doing great in the school of ministry, then suddenly emotionally crash and binge eat, or do these odd detoxes and hide out in her room for days. Lisa had been through a rehab program as a teen and had been sober for over a year. She'd knocked the giant of addiction out with a stone but did not cut its head off. It was quite the rollercoaster as she frantically tried to outrun her giant.

After a little over a year of living with us, Lisa's family giant started to rise up daily in her life. The pull of familiarity and what feels comfy is so strong. Do you know that scripture where Jesus says, *"For when a strong man is fully armed and guards his palace, his possessions are safe—until someone even stronger attacks and overpowers him, strips him of his weapons, and carries off his belongings" (Luke 11:21-22)*? That's a giant, and that's a real thing. We have personally experienced it and seen it dozens of times. Soon, Lisa was pulled back to the area of the country where her family lived, and she fell back into her old lifestyle, comfy and cozy with her family giant.

A year or so passed, and Lisa moved back to the area of our church, thinking she had left the giant behind. She would attend church sporadically but was constantly tormented by the jeers of her giant. After she gave birth to a beautiful baby, she went through another season of knocking that giant down; however, after less than a year, he was back, and his plot was to kill or destroy (see John 10:10). This was so difficult to watch as Lisa wrecked a few cars and was ticketed numerous times. She was making a decent living but living in absolute squalor.

Several of us were becoming quite concerned for her life and also for the life of her child. Her mom would come and stay a few weeks with her and help her get her house cleaned up, and Lisa would be back sober for a few weeks. Once her mom left and returned home, Lisa's path would quickly revert back to cowering at the feet of her comfy family giant of addiction.

One night, my husband and I got a call from one of Lisa's local family members who asked if we would help do an intervention, so we dropped everything and met them at her house. Her family members walked right in. There was no knocking, and that was awkward. We followed right behind. The house reeked of dirty dishes, trash, and booze. Lisa sat on the couch with a man none of us knew while her child played on a tablet on the floor. Lisa and the man were being extremely affectionate with each other.

My husband walked over and immediately introduced himself and shook that man's hand. They had met on a dating app, and this was one of the first times he had actually met Lisa in person. We told Lisa why we were there and that we were concerned for her safety and the safety of her child. The man asked straight up, "Is this an intervention?" We all simultaneously said "yes." Lisa was already intoxicated, so she just kind of laughed and agreed. We asked if her child could leave with the family members and said that we would be back in the morning to talk with her. She intoxicatingly complied.

The dating app guy left right after we did. Lisa drank herself to sleep, or at least to a passing out point; we were never quite sure on that one. One of her family members and I returned the next morning. Her apartment was a disaster. There were dead mice, trash, and dirty clothes, and the sink and kitchen counter were full of moldy dishes. We asked her if she was ready to get some help or if she was at least willing to allow her child to stay with relatives so he could be safe and have a stable atmosphere. Thankfully, she was ready for help.

We called around until we could find a place to take her for detox. Lisa didn't have insurance, so the pickings were slim and much more institutional. Her family members drove her there the next day for a seventy-two-hour detox. She could not have any external communication, and all of her personal belongings were locked up. After the three days, I went with her family member to pick Lisa up. The facility was in a downtown area that was quite impoverished, and the buildings were dilapidated and falling apart. Lisa came out looking completely different. In the car, she handed me her cell phone and told me the dating apps to delete, names of people to block, etc. She thanked us for fighting for her when she was not willing to fight for herself.

Lisa said, "I trust you two to do whatever is right for me and my child. I don't want to lose my child, and I don't want to die." It was at that point that Lisa had the sword in her hand to cut the giant's head off. We MUST surrender to God. We swing the sword, but it is in the name of the Lord that giants' heads roll and are defeated.

Lisa stayed with us while she worked through inpatient and outpatient rehab. She took the shot that keeps you from drinking. (Well, it makes you sick if you do drink.) She willingly signed up for the thirty-day rehab program and attended daily AA meetings. We attended her release ceremony from rehab, and Lisa gave a powerful speech to a room literally overflowing with people. She gave God all of the credit for her new life.

Lisa is four years sober at the date of writing this. She has married an amazing man of God who adores her child, and they have just had a beautiful baby. Some behaviors are still being modified, but the taunts of that family giant have been silenced. It was the same thing for Fred; he had to surrender and quit trying to do things his way. Jesus *is* the strongest man, and you have to keep Him as your savior and not try to do it yourself or put anyone or anything else in that position. Jesus—only Jesus!

I have one last story. Suicide is a fierce generational bear. It had run in my family for generations. When I was twelve, my fifteen-year-old brother took his own life. I was very young, so I don't recall what he was going through, and we all called it accidental until my mom passed away over forty years later. It's easy for that suicidal bear to come around after hibernating for years. It pops out and kills, and then it's masked as accidental. *Disclaimer:* Suicidal thoughts can be from mental illness also, and that may need medication and therapy. When my eldest son came back from serving in Iraq, he became quite tormented by that bear. He'd lost so many friends in the sands of the Middle East, all his battle buddies. There is guilt when you come home and others do not; plus, just trying to acclimate to civilian life is very challenging. I could discern that my son was struggling but was too subjective to help. My husband was deployed somewhere at that time too.

One night at church, I went to a retired military friend and asked him to pray for my son. He had slain many lions, bears, and giants in his own life and for others. That night, he prayed with my son fervently for quite some time. It felt like hours had gone by. That night, Jesus came close, and the tormenting bear was gone. My son is now happily married and has a beautiful wife and daughter. He loves God, loves his family, and serves faithfully at their church.

If you're not in a community with strong warriors, I emphatically recommend that you find one. There are too many battles in life to be alone. God is a good, good Father. Our walk of faith takes us through seasons in life: some mountain tops and some valleys. We need a tribe of people to stand with us on this journey. Also, it's important to have a mentor, spouse or pastor to vigilantly help you watch your back so that the lions, bears, or giants don't prowl around and try to sneak back into our lives. We need each other. I need my tribe!

Momistry is about setting a path for our children and grandchildren to walk in "lavished unfailing love for a thousand generations." We conquer lions, bears, and giants so our children do not have to, so they can have abundant lives full of the favor and goodness of God. They will have seasons too, but nothing that a quick giant-slaying won't take care of. Quick is important. In the account of David and Goliath, the Israelites had been taunted by Goliath for forty days. The longer you let the giant taunt, the more intimidation, fear, and acceptance start to sneak in. We fight for our legacy, and we train and help our children to fight as well.

> **But I lavish unfailing love for a thousand generations on those who love me and obey my commands.**
> **—Exodus 20:6**

## Momming is the best job ever and the hardest job ever. YOU CAN DO IT!

## Prayer:

*Father God, please open my eyes to see any bears, lions, or giants in my life. Jesus, come and help me to break these destructive things off of my family. Jesus, Your name is above any other name. You have and You will defeat anything that's not of You in my life and in the lives of my children and my grandchildren, unto a thousand generations. May my family and I experience Your lavish and unfailing love. As for me and my house, we choose to serve You, God, and to walk in Your commands. We choose blessing and life.*

# Practical points and questions:

1. Identify some family patterns or curses that you see still tormenting your family.
2. What are some bears or lions that you have already killed and eliminated their influence and impact?
3. Ask a pastor, mentor, counselor, or your spouse to help you see blindspots.
4. Do you personally have any giants in your life that you are comfortable with? Here are some examples: pornography, addiction, gluttony, narcissism, etc.
5. Can you see generational behaviors in your adult children? If so, how can you start praying, fasting, and fighting for them and for their children?

# Notes:

# CHAPTER 7

## How Do People Afford Children?

> **Money is only a tool. It will take you wherever you wish, but it will not replace you as the driver.**
>
> **Ayn Rand**

Diapers, formula, clothes, daycare, doctor's visits, co-pays, medicine, soaps for babies, lotions for babies: The list goes on and on. I was so excited to come home from the hospital with my firstborn. Well, I was excited and scared. He was the first baby in the family since I was born, and I was twenty-two. No one warned me about all of the expenses. Thirty-plus years ago, the hospitals encouraged formula feeding in order to make sure the baby was getting all the nutrients they needed. Looking back, I wonder, considering the price of formula, if they were in cahoots with the formula industry. Here's an interesting side note: Last time I went to visit my dad in California, they had the formula locked up in a case at the grocery store, like the nice jewelry counter or expensive perfume. You literally had to have an employee come with a key to get the formula out for you, and I was shocked. I couldn't help but ask myself, "Were people stealing formula?"

In the survey we did of moms and moms-to-be, "budget" was the fourth biggest concern, with 38% of mommas selecting it, and understandably so. We also know that finances are in the top five causes of disagreement in marriages, while raising children tops the list. The struggle is real. We certainly had our fair share of disagreements and downright blow-ups over both of those topics in our twenty-five years of marriage, especially as a blended family.

Money is also important to God. Jesus spoke about money frequently: Matthew 6:21, Matthew 19:21, Matthew 6:24, Luke 3:14,

Matthew 21:12, Matthew 12:41-44, Revelation 3:17, Luke 14:28, Matthew 13:22, and that's just to name a few. How you handle money is a good gauge on where your heart is. Well, it was for me. I was a worrier and came from a long family line of people who worry. It took years for me to learn to trust God in this area, hence the early marital discord. If I was going to be in the Momistry and raise healthy kids body, soul, and spirit, I was going to have to take a hard look at unhealthy family patterns and do some real self-reflection.

If you need help in the area of budgeting or understanding finances and how money works, read some of Dave Ramsey's books or listen to his podcasts. He keeps it simple and easy to understand. We definitely used some of his teachings to break bad habits, mostly for me. As I've mentioned before, after being raised in poverty and occasional lack, I had some wrong mindsets, control issues, and downright bad attitudes that needed to be renewed.

> **For where your treasure is, there your heart will be also.**
> **—Matthew 6:21 NIV**

My husband was the opposite. He liked to use a lot of credit, and his mind needed to be renewed in that area. He would confess to you that he still struggles some today in the area of credit. We didn't have credit cards when I was growing up, as my mom and her husband(s) couldn't get a line of credit anywhere. When I was eighteen years old and living on my own while working full time, I opened a small credit line at JCPenney's. My mom was so proud of me, like I'd hit the lottery—which, again, is such an unhealthy perspective.

Whether you come from a history of lack, abundance, or using too much credit, find some resources or a financial counselor to help get your mind renewed. When you see money the way that God sees money and you use it wisely, it is life changing. Most people need help in this area, so don't allow shame or pride to hold you back. A financial mentor is so helpful. Get some financial tools for your toolbelt.

> **A budget is telling your money where to go instead of wondering where it went.**
> **—Dave Ramsey**

One thing that really helped us was sitting down and writing a budget. I know it sounds super simple, but neither one of us had been doing that when we got married. We started a few years into our marriage, when we sat in a class at church where budgeting was mentioned. A written budget was a powertool in our toolbelt. Some tools, like a budget for us, are so powerful that they completely change the trajectory of your life. We still have one today. It's an Excel spreadsheet that my husband set up (because Excel is my least favorite program ever) that I can maneuver through. There are also apps and templates, and some people still use a pen and paper (which is crazy, I know). Seeing the numbers in print that showed where we were overspending and lacking was so helpful. We learned to trim the fat where needed.

OH, MY! This was not easy for me. I had such a bad attitude and control issues. I had the fear of not having enough and a whole gamut of poverty mindsets. It took years for my mind and attitude to be renewed. I knew I did not want to pass poverty down to my children. I mean, we were following a budget, and I was still very snarky about it. The sooner you start, the sooner the change starts. God wants you and your family to be prosperous.

The first few years we were married, we moved our little blended family to The Noel Farm in Bronaugh, MO. This is a rural town in Missouri, population 212. Our in-laws were so gracious to let us stay in the old

> **For I know the plans I have for you, declares the Lord, plans to prosper you and not to harm you, plans to give you hope and a future.**
> **—Jeremiah 29:11 NIV**

farmhouse rent-free for a few years. Okay, you Joanna Gaines ladies, this was *not* that type of farmhouse. The renters that had been in there before us had numerous dogs, had dressed (not in clothes) a deer in the entryway, and there were wasp nests all over the ceilings. The bathrooms were filthy, the kitchen counters and sinks were disgusting, there were dead mice in the closets and in the insulation on the oven, and there wasn't any central air conditioning. Central heat was propane and was only vented downstairs and not in the bedrooms upstairs. There was no garbage disposal (though we added one later) and no trash service (we used a burn barrel). The water was rich in minerals but tasted and smelled like sulfur. This California girl did not know what she was getting into; however, looking back, I wouldn't trade that season of my life for anything.

It was in that farmhouse that we started homeschooling some of our kids. It's also where our youngest son was born. It was where we decided that we were going to choose to do things differently and blaze a new trail for our family and break off destructive family patterns. It's where I quit my job to become a stay-at-home mom and enlisted in the Momistry. Before that, I had been the major breadwinner. Momming full time was not something that had EVER been on my radar, not once in my whole life. I have another confession: I used to mock women who stayed at home and homeschooled. Shame on me. This was one of the best seasons of my life, but also one of the hardest.

The farm is where we lived when we were not living on a written budget. One time, a family member had come for a few days to stay and was doing some laundry. She asked me where the fabric softener sheets were, and I told her, "We can't afford them." She later asked for paper towels, and I answered, "We can't afford them." We didn't have a written budget yet, so money was not in its proper place. Here is a tool for your toolbelt: When money is in its proper place, it is much more empowering to say "It's not in the budget" than it is to say "We can't afford it." A written budget helped us learn to tell money what to do and quit letting it tell us what to do. It has been a powertool.

Thankfully our children were young when we lived at the farm. Now they describe the season at the farm as magical, and some of their most fun childhood memories were made there. Apparently they didn't mind all of the peanut butter and jelly sandwiches, hot dogs, beans and rice, and rice and beans. They also talk about always having bread and butter with every meal, as cheap bread and margarine were good fillers. We still talk about a time when there was an ice storm and the power was out for three days. We all slept in front of the huge brick fireplace. We played board games by candlelight and cooked food on the camp stove by the back door. We boiled water on the camp stove, too, for baths. Those are priceless life memories. It could've been a hard time, but we made it a memory.

Children don't really remember the meals eaten; they remember the time sitting together around the table. Well, it's that way for young children anyway. My adult children remember meals now, and we are in the season of intentionally having weekly meals for our family gatherings. Your food and grocery budget is one area that you can somewhat control. Remember that time with the family is important, not fancy food or paper towels.

Our children ate so many PB&Js on cheap white bread with store brand peanut butter and jelly. When I was growing up, it was bologna and cheese on cheap white bread. I think this generation (Millennials and Gen Z) might get too hung up on food sometimes. Unless you had Celiac disease twenty years ago, you would never have heard of gluten-free. Now you go to a birthday party, and the cupcakes are gluten-free—if there are cupcakes at all. Some mommas are just having party-themed fruit cups or veggie bowls. I get it! We want to raise healthy kids, but if you're breaking your bank trying to keep up with trends, take three deep breaths and reevaluate. Is this for their health or for an image? Do you only eat healthy food? Hey, if you are vegan or if your child has severe allergies or you're a super health-conscious person, then you do you. But if you're just trying to be trendy, then this is an area you can definitely look at in your budget.

> **Children are sponges—they are going to absorb whatever is around them, so we need to be intentional about what surrounds them.**
> —Dave Ramsey, *Smart Money Smart Kids: Raising the Next Generation to Win with Money*

If you're looking for quality time or some healthy learning activities to do with children, it is possible. Here's a quick list of some practical, educational, and fun things to do that are inexpensive or free:

- Go for a walk in your neighborhood, and do a scavenger hunt (see Pinterest for a gazillion ideas).
- Picnic at the park. There are scavenger hunts for the park, too.
- Go for a hike.
- Go for a bike ride.
- Pick up sidewalk chalk, bubbles, balls, coloring books, or jacks and such from the dollar store.
- Have a board game night with popcorn.
- Watch a documentary and have everyone take notes and share what they learned.
- Start gardening. You could pick up seeds and dirt or sprouted plants from a chain store. Some cities have a community garden program.
- Read a biography together; you can take turns reading, depending on age and interest. Don't force a child to do something that they don't want to, but you can reward readers. Discuss highs and lows and takeaways from the book. Our family read *Bruchko* together when we lived in the farmhouse.
- Play with water balloons and squirt guns. If you don't like guns, you can use empty dish soap containers or shampoo bottles.
- Bake, cook, or paint. My daughter and I did latch hook rugs. Model cars are another option.

If all else fails, use Google or Pinterest for more ideas. You could also have a jar with ideas written down on pieces of papers which someone draws randomly, which can help deter any possible conflict on the activity. Our kids loved board games, and we would get cheap buckets of vanilla or chocolate ice cream for our treat. Sometimes we would stir crushed cookies or candy bars into the ice cream. Whatever you do, do it together. That is the point.

Our family has gone through seasons of buying brand new clothes and seasons of shopping thrift stores and wearing hand-me-downs. We have also had vacations where we camped in a tent and others where we spent days on Chesapeake Bay and Waikiki Beach, Hawaii. Don't get weary of doing good, and don't give up. *"So let's not get tired of doing what is good. At just the right time we will reap a harvest of blessings if we don't give up." (Galatians 6:9)* It's not about the expense; it's about quantity and quality time. It does not have to be expensive, so don't go into debt for experiences—some of the best ones are around the table playing a game of Life by candlelight, because the power went out in an ice storm.

When we had our youngest son, I was on Medicaid and WIC. We occasionally got food from our church food pantry. If you're in a season of need, don't be too prideful or ashamed to ask for help; that's what it's for. Just don't set up camp there. Keep moving out of lack into prosperity. God wants us to prosper (see Jeremiah 29:11). In this season of our lives, we get to buy the young family sitting across the restaurant from us dinner or give a holy handshake (a handshake where you inconspicuously hand someone money) or send a Target delivery of diapers and baby items to a new mommy. DON'T GIVE UP!

Being slow to respond and not quick to react financially was huge for us, too. Before our minds were renewed, we would purchase a vehicle based on the monthly payment amount. Now, we purchase a car based on its practicality and price. We don't have to have it. Seriously, the feeling of having to have something is much more powerful than the feeling of needing to. Need is the healthy filter.

One example is when my daughter needed braces. We went and got free consultations from orthodontists with timelines and prices. The range was *huge*, from $5,000 for 5 years to $1,800 for 24 months (which ended up being only 18 months). I also watched a little boy for several months or worked part time retail to balance the budget. Another time, I took a job at a daycare where I could take my youngest child to work with me. We have sold furniture and old jewelry for some extra cash. With Facebook Marketplace, it is so easy these days. You can make a list of ideas for balancing the budget so that you have a backup plan if needed. That is not fear; that is good planning. We are to be wise as serpents and gentle as doves: *"So be as shrewd as snakes and harmless as doves" (Matthew 10:16b)*. Also, plan for the cost before building: *"But don't begin until you count the cost. For who would begin construction of a building without first calculating the cost to see if there is enough money to finish it?" (Luke 14:28)*.

There were years where I did not buy any new clothes for myself, didn't get a pedicure, didn't eat in a restaurant that didn't have a dollar menu, didn't have a GNO (girls' night out), didn't go to conferences, and so on. I have zero regrets, not one. My regret would be not always living in the moment with my children.

Too many times I was distracted by circumstances and civilian affairs. *"Soldiers don't get tied up in the affairs of civilian life, for then they cannot please the officer who enlisted them." (2 Timothy 2:4)* I was there but not there, if you know what I mean. I had to learn to turn off everything else and savor the moments. They really do go by so fast. That's a tool for your toolbelt, mommas: Be in the moment. Enjoy the snuggles, giggles, loud singing, playing, and messes. My first favorite daughter-in-love (as I call our eldest son's wife) once said, "Don't mind the mess.

We are making memories." Now I hear myself saying that when my grandson brings in a handful of sand from the sand table and rubs it into the carpet or when my granddaughter dumps three puzzles out and plays with them for about three minutes and walks away, leaving twenty pieces on the table. More messes means more memories.

There's a saying about leaving a legacy for your children: "Let our ceiling be their floor." We want them to start where we left off, so make sure you're leaving something that's growing and flourishing. When my mom passed away, she had nothing. Seriously, she had not one asset to her name. There was a small life insurance policy that covered her funeral, but my husband and I had to cover a lot of her end-of-life expenses. You do not want that for your children, so plan *now*!

One thing that really helped me was to get a small notebook and start tracking every penny I spent, literally every cent. Each grocery store trip, gas station stop, or late night ice cream run was written down. Of course, gas in the car and groceries are a priority; however, $20 ice cream at 9PM is not healthy for the budget (or my weight). If you're struggling with worrying and feeling like your finances are out of control, like you have a hole in your pocket, try keeping a log. That was sure helpful

> **You have planted much but harvest little. You eat but are not satisfied. You drink but are still thirsty. You put on clothes but cannot keep warm. Your wages disappear as though you were putting them in pockets filled with holes. —Haggai 1:6**

for me to see where I was being frivolous. I was able to take back control. A $5 Starbucks drink five times a week, fifty-two weeks a year is $1,300. Also, come on, who just gets coffee? We get egg bites or pumpkin or banana bread, or we say, "It's okay, it's the protein balls." Get a log!

This might step on some toes, but can we talk about extracurricular activities for children? These can be very expensive and time consuming. Make sure your child and you are ready for the commitment. Otherwise, save your money. We recently did three months of voice lessons for our twelve-year-old daughter. She has a karaoke machine and loves to sing. She also loves singing and worshiping at church. She did great for the first month. Daily practice was required, and it was scales and voice warmup, not a lot of singing. She would do it faithfully as soon as she got home from school. She would briefly do the assigned practice then jump on her karaoke machine. By the second month, I was having to remind her every day. She did it but was no longer enjoying it. During the last month, she rarely practiced, and it was usually just the hour before her lesson. We stopped after three months and will revisit the idea when *she* is ready to make the commitment.

Sports sound so fun—until it's huge team fees, health checks, uniforms, and special gear, and then there are games on Saturday at 7AM and practice three nights a week in addition to homework. The discipline that they learn is awesome, as well as camaraderie and teamwork. There are some priceless character lessons that can be learned. Always remember that your Momistry is to keep them safe: body, soul, and spirit. If there is a chance that they might make sports or gymnastics or whatever it is an idol in their lives, be very careful. In reality most twenty-four-year-olds do not still compete in gymnastics, volleyball, or basketball. Most don't even play sports for fun at that age. Our long-term goal should be that they are still loving and serving Jesus. Choose wisely!

In addition to a budget, early on in our marriage we decided to be tithers. I know this is an uber sensitive subject for some, but God was and is so faithful to us. We wanted to be faithful to Him and obey His word. I have a confession: I was not really thrilled about this at first and resisted the idea. I was definitely raised in a paycheck-to-paycheck household, and we lacked often. After seeing God be so faithful to us in this area, I'm now a firm believer that you want God involved in your finances. His provision is limitless. Tithing was another powertool for us. Here are a few scriptures you can meditate on: 2 Chronicles 31:4-5, Deuteronomy 12:6, Genesis 14:20, Leviticus 27:30-34, Matthew 23:23, Mark 12:41-44 and Malachi 3:8-12. It took some time for me to be free in the area of giving to God *first*. I had decades of baggage of living in poverty, control, and worry. For my husband, as soon as we heard the teaching on tithing, he wanted to jump right in. God has always taken great care of us—always!

> **Physical training is good, but training for godliness is much better, promising benefits in this life and in the life to come.**
> **—1 Timothy 4:8**

Off the top of my head, I can recall numerous times when God showed Himself as our provider. One was when we didn't have a running vehicle, and someone just gave us a car. Another year, before budget living but after tithing, my husband lost his job a month before Christmas, and someone from our church left hundreds of dollars of gifts on our porch for our children. I'm talking about gifts like a bike, large remote-control vehicles, LEGO sets, and such. There have been, and still are (including one just last week!), so many unexpected checks, deposits into our bank account, scholarships out of nowhere, furniture given to us, someone buying our meal at a restaurant, or someone randomly handing us cash (a holy handshake), etc. My dad would randomly offer to help, or my in-laws would. The list is long. We began tithing out of obedience to what God had said in His Word and to us. It was not from any external pressure or person, and He has shown Himself faithful.

We taught our children about tithing too. They are all pretty generous, so it wasn't a fight. Sometimes they would just give all of the money in their pocket or purse to someone or in a church offering. Our children are watching how we handle our money and seeing if we are generous or greedy. As they get older, they will comprehend what God says and what we do. Start working out finances now, so you can set a powerful example for your children.

Years ago, a single mother at our church was immediately given kinship placement of her two young nephews. Kinship placement is like foster care, but you are related to the child. They showed up at her door in dirty clothes, each of them having a green trash bag with a few clothes and blankets. Our youngest son was right in between their two ages. When he heard that they didn't have any toys, he went into his room so upset for them. He scrambled around in there for a bit and finally came out. He said, "Mom, I want to give them some of my toys." I said, "That's so generous, buddy. Do you want to get a bag and take it to them?" He looked at me perplexed and said, "No, come here. I'll show you." We walked down the hall into his room, and his toy box was pulled out with a small pile of toys next to it. I gestured towards the small pile and said, "Go get a bag for those, and we can take them over to them." My son looked at the pile and then me and said, quite frankly, "Mom, that pile is for me to keep. The toy box is for them." The toy box was a very large, solid wooden box that a family member had made for our oldest son a decade before, and it was still quite full. It was much too heavy and large for me, so he and his daddy took it over to them that evening. The aunt of the two boys wept.

In this generation, maybe it's the lack of priorities that is keeping some younger people from tithing. Put God *first*! There are plenty of teachings out there on it. When talking with young mommas, I hear them complain about not having money but then see social media posts of them eating dinner out four to five nights a week or going to the movies in a theater. So many think that they need a Starbucks coffee every day when they have gourmet coffee, a coffee pot, flavored syrups, creamers, and frothers at home. When we start being doers of the word and not just hearers, it looks and sounds differently. *"But don't just listen to God's word. You must do what it says. Otherwise, you are only fooling yourselves." (James 1:22)* God really is into prospering His people. We simply have to put Him *first*!

There's no need to worry about the cost of having children. You can afford them. There is a high price when having them (for the birth), but they are worth every single cent. *"I've never seen the righteous forsaken or their children begging for bread." (Psalms 37:25 NIV)* Know that whatever the need is, God will come through. He is a good Father who loves to bless His children. His blessings are needs and not always wants. God sees the big picture of your Momistry, and we must learn to trust Him and lean not on our own understanding (see Proverbs 3).

## Momming is the best job ever and the hardest job ever. YOU CAN DO IT!

## Prayer:

*Father God, help me learn to be a good steward. You have blessed my life, and I want to be a blessing to my family and to those around me. Holy Spirit, help me embrace God's way of handling my finances. Help me to trust You as my Provider. Empower me to take back control over my finances and to start using money as a tool. Soften my heart to this topic as I surrender control to You. Thank You, God, for Your ways are higher than mine. Amen.*

## Practical points and questions:

1. What do you think about tithing and why? Are your thoughts based on fear or faith?
2. Are you using a budget for your monthly expenses?
3. What are some areas where you know you can start managing spending better?
4. Do you need extra income? Brainstorm some ideas.
5. Are you struggling with patterns of control, lack or poverty from your childhood?
6. Does your view of debt need to be renewed?

## Notes:

# CHAPTER 8

# What Do Healthy Boundaries Look Like?

> **My boundaries are a fence with a gate. They're built to keep the people inside of my fence safe.**

This is such a hot topic in this generation. When my older children were young, you never even heard the word boundaries. Now there are so many books, podcasts, blogs, and even sermons about it. It was something we had to learn to start addressing about twenty years ago. At that time, we didn't have many tools to work with, so it was a lot of trial and error and learning along the way. It wasn't easy, but it was life changing.

As a wife, mom, Christian, sister, friend, employee, and all the other hats we wear, it is easy to get pulled in so many different directions. It can be exhausting and exasperating. The first thing you have to do is pick what is most important to you and your family. I've watched way too many moms choose ministry over family and then reap a harvest of children not serving Jesus. I've seen other moms get burned out on trying to do everything and quit church altogether, again resulting in grown children not serving the Lord. Also, numerous wives get off course with a career, ministry, or even education and end up shipwrecked in life. We need boundaries in our lives. I like to say, "My boundaries are a fence with a gate. They're built to keep the people inside of my fence safe." You and your spouse are the gatekeepers of your fence. That's what boundaries are.

Stop and close your eyes for a moment. See yourself, your kids, your spouse, your pets, your home, etc. Next, draw an invisible perimeter around them in your mind. That is your boundary, your fence. My dear friend Diane can walk through my gate any time. She even has an invisible key. She can come and go as she pleases. The mentally ill grown man who went off of his medicine and showed up on our doorstep is walked to his car by my husband. If my husband was not home, I would not answer the door. My Momistry is to keep my children safe: body, soul, and spirit. I love the man and pray for him, but the help that he needs is not inside my fence. I hope that gives you a helpful and healthy perspective on boundaries.

I want to interject here that fences are not walls, and fences have gates. While there may be times you have to lock someone out to be safe, there also may one day be healing and reconciliation. That doesn't mean free access to your gate. It just means that you took the lock off. Jesus is a rescuer, and He radically changes people. Walk in forgiveness (see Luke 6:37), keep your hands clean and your heart pure (see Psalms 24:3-4), and listen to guidance from the Holy Spirit (see John 16:13). That's what's helped me.

Being a good gatekeeper will help your family on their journey of faith and life. A wise pastor friend once said, "A small rudder steers a ship, and with the slightest wrong turn, it can slowly take you completely off course." Take some time with your spouse (if you have one), and prayerfully consider what is most important to you. After that, if you haven't already, WRITE IT DOWN (see Habakkuk 2:2)! This is vital to keeping your ship going in the right direction. It also helps with setting boundaries and managing the gates of your time and relationships.

> **When the Spirit of truth comes, he will guide you into all truth. He will not speak on his own but will tell you what he has heard. He will tell you about the future.**
> **—John 16:13**

When we wrote these family priorities down, we called it our mission statement. We prayed and let the Holy Spirit guide us. This wasn't a one-and-done thing; it has changed as seasons have changed in our lives. The one goal that never changed was that we will love God and love people. This was a tool that we picked up much later in life, but it was so important.

> Then Jesus said to his disciples, 'If any of you wants to be my follower, you must give up your own way, take up your cross, and follow me. If you try to hang on to your life, you will lose it. But if you give up your life for my sake, you will save it. And what do you benefit if you gain the whole world but lose your own soul? Is anything worth more than your soul?'
> —Matthew 16:24-26

The Noel Family mission statement that helped establish healthy boundaries looks/looked something like this:

*We love God with all of our hearts, minds, souls, and strength, and we worship Him only.*

*Family is first. We will love, respect, and serve one another.*

*We will love God and love people, all people.*

*Our church is our community. We will love and honor its leaders. We will serve however we are needed.*

*Home is our sanctuary, and we will treat it as such. Our doors are open to those in need as long as it is safe. Our family has enough love that we can share with others. Our home is a safe place and a judgment-free zone. Love covers!*

When you write it in order of priority, it is easier to make decisions and say "yes" or "no" to something. For example, if a child has a school or sporting event, family is before church, so you may occasionally have to miss church for a game, play, or recital. Warning: I've also seen several families stop serving Jesus to serve sports, theater, or dance. These parents then have kids who can do a wonderful dance or throw a touchdown or pitch 80 MPH, but they stop serving and loving Jesus. Remember that Momistry is keeping your children safe: body, soul, and spirit. What good is it if they are a star quarterback or gymnast if they don't love God and are losing their souls (see Matthew 16:26)? It sounds harsh (sorry not sorry), but it's true; however, I have also seen families balance this well and attend games and take children to practices but be back in church on Sunday. Their children also still attend youth groups, VBS, and church camps, keeping God as their first priority. These families have healthy boundaries. It is not about church attendance as a religious duty. It's about our *first* priority. God rescued me, He saved my family, He created the universe, and He overwhelms us with His love, so we worship Him and thank Him and praise His name. He is our top priority!

Putting God first is imperative to keeping your ship going in the right direction. That is not the same as ministry or serving in your church, so this is where boundaries are needed. This was such a struggle for me. I'm a closet people pleaser and want to do everything. Even today at times, my adult children will tell

> For marriage to last, it has to be built on a much greater purpose than the happiness and well-being of two single people. That purpose has to be greater than any amount of stress and struggle that comes into the marriage.
> —Jimmy Evans

me, "Mom you need to say 'no'" or "Do you want me to call and tell them 'no'?" Ouch! I have said "no" to ministry trips, speaking engagements, leading this or that, and helping this person or child. Even when "Patty, pastor so-and-so has asked me to call you and see if you would…" was the approach. That one was really hard for someone with father rejection issues. Priorities are important! It's okay to say "no" to anything that tries to jump your fence, kick open your gate, or trump your mission statement. BE FREE TO SAY "NO!" That one is for any other closet people pleasers.

Sometimes you have to set boundaries with bosses too. Something I hear in this generation is "Take ownership," while the owner of the business is reaping all of the profits and sprinkling occasional coins to the employees. One of my sons got a call from his boss on a weekend evening during *his* family birthday party while we were all at the table eating the dinner he had selected. Yep, he stepped away and took the call. I'm sure his and his boss's ears were burning from the lashing they took at the table from his siblings, their spouses, and his parents. He and I had some straight talk the next day. He had stepped outside of our family boundaries. Of course, he knew it immediately when he took the call. He got some chiding from his siblings upon returning to his birthday dinner table, too. Employers are a difficult one, especially when it is the source that God uses to provide for your family; however, Jesus' death was enough for your boss, so you don't have to sacrifice your family.

Remind people that boundaries are for you, not for them. They're to manage what you have prioritized. "I'm sorry I missed your call. It was my birthday dinner with my family, so I silenced my phone for three hours." A smile and a hug go a *long* way. Smiling and saying, "No, my child cannot stay at your house overnight. We don't do sleepovers right now," puts it on you as the parent and not on the child. It's important that your children never feel the brunt of your family boundaries. Again, this is for your family, and you are not obligated to anyone else. You're obligated to God and your family, and that's it, so be free to kindly tend to the fence around them.

Listen, I realize I say "kindly and gently," but there might be time for firmly and loudly or even restraining orders. Safety is the issue! *"Do all that you can to live in peace with everyone." (Romans 12:18)* If you've done all you can, then you've done all you can. When your children or you do not feel safe, then you do what the Holy Spirit leads you to do, and that's usually to get help. Abuse is physical, sexual, emotional, and neglect. If you or your children are experiencing *any* of those, seek a pastor, police, or local abuse center for help. I'm a momma bear, and most of the time, I'm gentle, kind, and loving; however, if you mess with my children, grandchildren, children in my care, or people in my care, I can rip your head off and spoon out your lungs—with love of course. I love you enough to teach you that crossing my fence and safety boundaries is not okay, ever.

After reading a few books and listening to a couple of podcasts, I wrote down some paraphrased sentences to help me. Writing them down was a huge help. I'd even put sticky notes on the fridge or use a dry erase marker on my bathroom mirror. For some practical tools, here are a few of those if you need them:

- I'm sorry, but I have another commitment that day.
- Lunch doesn't work for me Tuesday, but I can do an hour coffee date on Friday morning.

- Thank you so much for the invite. God has me focusing my energy in a different direction right now. Have so much fun though. I'll miss you all.
- I love spending time with you; however, I'm working on a big project right now. Can you please reach back out to me in three months?

Once you get a few of those down, it helps with managing your fence and boundary line. Sometimes people will get upset or try to manipulate, gaslight, or guilt trip you. Explain, "This is what works best for me." You can even apologize, but hold your line. "I'm so sorry, but this is what works best for me." This might happen with close friends or family too.

In family or friend gatherings you can say, "When you sit by my daughter, it makes her uncomfortable. I'm sure you understand that she is young and has a lot of feelings going on, and her feeling safe is my first priority." Listen, this situation might also be "when you hug my daughter" or "talk to my son." You're not responsible for someone else's feelings, so be prepared to hold your ground with, "This wasn't really a negotiation. Again, my job is to make sure my child feels safe. Thank you for your understanding."

My mom's third husband would sit too close to my eldest daughter when she was ten or eleven years old and touch her legs. She would get up and move, and he would follow her. I spoke to him kindly (this was before I had sharpened my momma bear claws), and he continued to do it. My daughter mentioned that it was making her very uncomfortable. This was my family, so I spoke to him again. Usually, the plan is if it's my family, I talk to them, and if it's my husband's family, he talks to them. I also talked to my mom, as this was her husband. He continued to follow my daughter around, and it was weird and started to get creepy. Right after the last incident where I spoke to him, he did it again at my mom's home. My husband was there, and he immediately walked up and said, "[Third husband's name], come see our new tires on the van." While outside, the third husband heard very directly and clearly from my husband, who is 6'4" and at the time was in the military. I'm not sure what was said, but that man rarely ever even spoke to my eldest daughter again.

On occasion, you may have to use firmer tactics. One of my relatives would constantly call me about their financial problems. They had a history of decades of poor financial decisions (my whole life) and chose to continue making them. We had helped them numerous times. We walked them through Dave Ramsey to the point of being out of debt *with* an emergency fund and a savings account. After they returned to their previous patterns, when this person called, I would feel obligated to help or would feel guilty if I didn't. It would cause me great concern, sometimes for days. After numerous attempts of me trying to set a boundary of us no longer helping them and them not talking to me about it, it continued. We had helped them to the tune of tens of thousands of dollars. Finally, my husband sat my family member down and lovingly explained my heart to always help them and how we couldn't any longer and how upset it was making me. He closed by telling them that if they wanted to continue to be able to call me and to be invited to family events, then they needed to respect our boundaries, and they did.

My husband also had to talk to a family member who kept showing up to school events, wedding/baby showers, and birthday parties very drunk. They would be extremely loud and use foul language and sometimes even physically stumble. The boundary kept getting broken, so sadly, we are no longer able to invite this person to events, and that was their choice, not ours. Our children had been embarrassed on several occasions and did not feel safe. We also have an agreement that if we show up to a gathering and they are there drunk, then we leave. This is a well-informed person who has had family interventions and professional interventions several times. Alcoholism runs in their family. You cannot get free from demons that you enjoy and invite in.

I have a confession: I do much better setting boundaries with an acquaintance or stranger. When it comes to family, I can be way too subjective. My husband has to help me be objective. We all need an objective voice. Sometimes my objectivity can also come from my adult children.

One election season, I was getting pulled into tons of political rhetoric. It was toxic and knocked me way off course. I was even sharing sarcastic, divisive, and hurtful memes and articles on social media. My content is usually encouraging, hopeful, or family pics. My middle, adult son asked me for some coffee time. Some of my favorite moments in my life happened during heart talks over coffee in our lanai. I made us espressos in large ceramic mugs, making sure the milk was perfectly frothed. We sat and casually chatted for a bit. He rambled about cryptocurrency and then data analytics, and I nodded regularly with an occasional "That sounds awesome" and "Wow, I'm so proud of you" and "Yes." Please note that I still have very limited understanding of either of those topics, but it is a millennial thing, and I enjoy listening to him talk.

After a bit of chitchat, he asked me, "Have you heard of confirmation bias?" I answered, "No, I have not." He began very lovingly explaining it to me. In a nutshell, it's when you surround yourself with people who just say the same things you say and believe the same way you do, so it's all you know. He also shared that the algorithms of social media and news sources and such then spoon feed you that content. WHAT! I felt slightly violated but also convicted. I had surrounded myself, if I can respectfully say, with white, middle- and upper- class, Republican Evangelicals. This is exactly the tight, little box I would fit in; however, in that box, I was not hearing the how's or why's of anyone else.

Listen, I could've easily brushed that conversation off—especially since it came from my son, who is half my age and has an education from an extremely liberal, left-wing, Ivy League type of college. I also could have ignored the Holy Spirit prodding me to open my eyes to the other 90% (loosely) of people whom He created in His image. Wow, just wow. My son reminded me of our commitment to loving people and that should not just be people who agree with me. We had a boundary in our family, and I had crossed it. Since then, I have had conversations with all kinds of different people and opened my mind and heart to them. This last election season, I didn't post one political post on any social media platform. I "snoozed" haters for months and even unfollowed a few divisive ones. I didn't respond to dozens of emails baiting me for political arguments. I did my research privately and voted accordingly.

You are the gatekeeper of healthy boundaries around you and your family. If you need

> **Boundaries are for you, not for the other person.**
> —Havilah Cunnington

more help in this area, there are several other amazing books on boundaries. I will list some in the back of the book for you. Sometimes I will still listen to podcasts and read blogs or listen to an audiobook to keep me on track. This section is just "Boundaries by Patty." If you need help in this area, find some more tools, then find an accountability person—someone who's a mentor, pastor, or maybe a therapist. This person is not usually someone in your family. Those tools really helped me.

**Momming is the best job ever and the hardest job ever.
YOU CAN DO IT!**

## Prayer:

*Holy Spirit, empower me to start setting boundaries for my family and for myself. I need to focus on the priorities that You have given me. Give me and my husband wisdom to write a mission statement. Show me any traps of man-pleasing or guilt trips, and let me respond with love and grace. Help me to be a wise gatekeeper. Thank you, God, for this powerful tool of making sure my time is spent on what You have called me to do. Amen.*

## Practical points and questions:

1. Do you have a family mission statement to help you set boundaries?
2. Do you struggle with putting a wall around you and your family instead of a fence with a gate? Check yourself for unforgiveness, clean hands, and a pure heart.
3. Who can you reach out to who can help hold you accountable to the boundaries that you set?
4. Can you identify any situations where you need to set firmer boundaries?
5. It can be helpful to identify people pleasing and/or guilt. Identify those if you have them.
6. Take a few moments and think about how boundaries can help you and your family, and make some notes.

# Notes:

# CHAPTER 9

## Oh, So Many Opinions with So Many Choices

> **Wise choices will watch over you. Understanding will keep you safe.**
>
> **Proverbs 2:11**

Certainly by now, as a parent or parent-to-be, you have heard advice and opinions from all types of people. This is especially true in a culture that is daily perusing the internet and social media, as some cannot put their phones down for even an hour-long church service. You no longer have to get cornered at church or at a family reunion by a young mom of two children under three who thinks that she knows everything and has experienced everything. Of course, that still happens too; that is a good opportunity to set a healthy boundary in person. You can simply say "Thank you for your opinion" or "I'll mention that to my husband. Thank you." and smile and walk away. Online, just keep scrolling, or if it's overwhelming, mute or hide that person. All you have to do nowadays is watch the stories and news feeds flooding the airways with strong opinions from every walk of parenting and life, most of them SAHMs with small children.

Some of the ways that I used to make wise decisions were prayer, the Bible, my mentor(s), and standing firm in what I already knew. Referring back to the suggestion in Chapter 3, I remind you about finding a mentor who's at least ten years older than you *and* has adult children and/or a life like you would like to have in ten-plus years. That will help you if you are struggling with confusion or are just plain emotionally exhausted. Also, that mission statement mentioned in the previous chapter will help you do what's best for *your* family. It will help you stick to *your* family plan. Remember that Momistry is keeping your child safe: body, soul, and spirit. Listen, I will probably step on a lot of toes in this chapter. My intention is not to offend any young moms. My heart is to equip them and to help them be set free to operate in their calling of Momistry, to minister to *their* children.

When my eldest son was born in California in 1987, the nurses didn't push breastfeeding. They encouraged formula feeding. They did this so you could monitor how much babies were eating and get the help you needed from others after just having had a baby.

> **Obviously, I'm not trying to win the approval of people, but of God. If pleasing people were my goal, I would not be Christ's servant.**
> **—Galatians 1:10**

Our nurses knew that I was going back to work, since in California, most households require two full time incomes because of the exorbitant cost of living. That may have played a role in the baby formula feeding too. There was no shaming from my peers because I formula fed in 1987 or 1991 or 1997. Yes, I formula fed all three of the babies I birthed. Guess what? They all turned out so awesome! They're all healthy, happy, thriving adults.

In 2021, I know young moms that hide containers of formula when friends come over, because they don't want to be judged. One was a young mom who was struggling with depression. Postpartum depression is a real deal. Please get help. Her milk supply was low, and after trying several different things, she started topping her breast milk bottles with formula. She said that it added to her mom-guilt to know that her body wouldn't work for her child.

Y'all are being ridiculous. Stop it. Just stop it. All of us moms want to do what's best for our babies. Sometimes that's formula and over-the-counter meds, and sometimes that's breastfeeding and all of the essential oils and herbal rubs you can imagine. Do your research, agree with the baby-daddy, and do what *you* think is right for your family. You're super smart. I mean, you're reading a book, so you can read and comprehend information. Beware of the lone doctor's article or some obscure country having results with whatever method, and stick with appointed experts, not self-appointed Facebook gurus who sometimes barely have a high school diploma. Do you know what? You also do not owe it to anyone to do a bunch of digging around if you already have personal convictions about how you want to feed your baby. *"Obviously, I'm not trying to win the approval of people, but of God. If pleasing people were my goal, I would not be Christ's servant." (Galatians 1:10)* God will not be bothered either way. BE FREE! To quote my pastor friend, "Will it matter in eternity?"

As I mentioned in the introduction, we have five children, and four are now adults. All five were given childhood vaccinations, and in 2021, that included some of them getting the COVID-19 vaccine (one is breast-feeding, so she's waiting). They are all healthy and happy, hardworking, independent, self-sufficient, well-educated, prosperous adults. (The twelve-year-old is still working on the hard-working and self-sufficient part.) Not one of my children ever had any kind of a reaction to a vaccine. No one in any of our families has ever had a reaction to a vaccine. We don't have any genetic or neurological issues that would cause us to question taking the recommended vaccines; however, we must respect those people who do have issues or who just choose not to vaccinate. This is America, people. We have freedom (sorry, Canadians and Australians).

No one's ever knocked on my door to vaccinate me or anyone in our home. Sheesh, we are COVID-vaccinated, and no one even asks to see our cards. I've been carrying them in my purse for months after all of the hype, and so far no one has asked to see them, not one person. On a side note, as mentioned before, my husband is retired military and has seen the effects of diseases in other countries where they don't have access to vaccines. I promise you that a mother in Nigeria holding her child covered in a rash and burning with a high fever from the measles covets your life in so many ways, and vaccines are just one of those ways. There are definitely medical reasons to avoid or delay vaccinations. If you're a worrier, you might want to do some research on this topic, but be free to make the choice that's best for you and your family. Keep in mind that there is still a group of people who think the earth is flat, and they have a lot of propaganda out there too. It all looks pretty convincing. If I wasn't a well-educated person, I might get my "It's Flat" hat with the rest of the flat-earthers. Again, do your research, then decide what's best for *your* family. God will not be bothered either way. BE FREE! Again, quoting one of my pastors, "Will it matter in eternity?"

The other day, my two daughters and I took two of the grandkids to the park. I held the baby (my favorite job) while everyone played and talked. I ended up talking with another couple of ladies, of which one was a grandma too, sitting at the picnic table next to us. They were speaking a different language but also spoke clear English. After a few minutes, my daughters and one of the young mommas with whom they

> **Do not judge others, and you will not be judged. Do not condemn others, or it will all come back against you. Forgive others, and you will be forgiven.**
> **—Luke 6:37**

connected came over to where I was. We were all chatting away. One young momma shared her fertility journey and how she had used doctors and medicine for both of her children. The ladies I had been talking with were listening intently. She then told us the awful things that some supposed "Christians" had said to her about fertility doctors not being of God and about her lack of faith. Her eyes filled with tears, and her voice cracked. It had been over four years, and she was still so wounded. I immediately responded, while touching her arm gently, "I'm so sorry that happened to you. Remember that religion is mean, and Jesus is gentle and humble, and His yoke is easy. He is all about relationships." She smiled back, and we visited for a while longer. Then the littles started getting fussy, so we got in our cars to leave.

We got in the car, and I cried. My heart was so broken for this woman who so desperately wanted to be a momma and, due to health reasons, was struggling to get pregnant. She enlisted the help of doctors and now has two beautiful children whom she adores. We must do better than this, ladies. If your child had diabetes, would you give them insulin to live? We should never question another person's faith walk—never. God is the judge, not us (see Luke 6:37). We are to love, encourage, empower, equip, pray, and believe good for others.

My eldest son and his wife struggle with infertility. If I weren't fifty-five years old, I'd offer to be their surrogate. We have all prayed, fasted and prayed, then prayed some more. Did God give them a miracle baby? Yes! Did God connect them with the right doctors? Also yes. Did they have peace with God when choosing IVF? Yes. Please note: I *will* go very momma bear on you if you say one word about lack of faith, Sarah and Hagar, Hannah or Elizabeth. In 2 Timothy 4:20, Paul says: "I left Trophimus sick in Miletus." Paul's shadow healed the sick, and cloths that he had touched were sent to people. With his anointing and their faith, those cloths brought healing, yet Trophimus was left sick.

God knit together my first beautiful, brilliant granddaughter, Maelee Marie, through His hands and the hands of doctors in her mommy's womb. People are given different graces. May I walk freely in mine, you walk freely in yours, and may we allow others to walk freely in theirs.

Along this same line of choices and opinions includes the birthing experience. Some ladies want to have their babies in their bathtubs at home with a doula. Others want to be in a hospital and have an epidural.

> **Religion is mean, and Jesus is gentle and humble, and His yoke is easy.**

What is right for one momma may not be right for another momma, and *that's okay*. Also, what you chose for baby number one at twenty-two might completely be different from baby number four at thirty-seven. Consider the possibility of complications, too. Momma, you do YOU!

Some mommas want their moms or a friend in the room when birthing, and others just want their spouse. Others want all of the guests and flowers and snacks and gifts, and others want just immediate family and are more private. Both are right! Do you think that God is in heaven shaking His head in disappointment at the mommy birthing in the hospital and that He's clapping for the one with the doula in the bathtub? Nope, He's cheering for every baby born and has a plan and purpose for each one of them, regardless of where or how they enter the world. Whatever you and your husband decide is right, *is* right, as long as it is Biblical.

A young woman asked me about disciplining children the other day. She had been raised in more of a spare-the-rod-and-spoil-the-child (see Proverbs 13:24) home. I was raised in the because-I-said-so era of parenting with a lot of yelling, ugly words, throwing things, slamming doors, and grounding. Now that I'm older, I think that this young lady just wanted my take on disciplining children in 2022.

> **For I know the plans I have for you, says the Lord. They are plans for good and not for disaster, to give you a future and a hope.**
> **—Jeremiah 29:11**

Here are my thoughts on the subject of disciplining children after thirty-four years of parenting. Keep in mind that this is after our early years of following teachings that leaned way too far on the discipline/rod/stoning Scriptures. Did you know that the Bible actually instructs parents to teach/counsel/train our children *twice* as many times as discipline is mentioned? Here's one of my favorites: *"And now a word to you parents. Don't keep on scolding and nagging your children, making them angry and resentful. Rather, bring them up with the loving discipline the Lord himself approves, with suggestions and godly advice." (Ephesians 6:4 TLB)*

Sadly, with our oldest son, we were new to parenting and applied the teachings that emphasized the rod. I specifically remember attending a parenting class where the rod Scriptures were taught and how the teachers suggested using a wooden spoon, because they didn't want you to spank your child with your hand, as you were punishing them to drive away foolishness. *"A youngster's heart is filled with foolishness but physical discipline will drive it far away." (Proverbs 22:15)* Also, they referenced Scriptures about stoning a rebellious child (see Deuteronomy 21:18-21). As I think back on those classes, my heart is grieved. There were so many of us young parents in the room just wanting help raising our children to love God and love their families.

We moms need to be making suggestions, giving godly advice, and disciplining *lovingly*. Mostly that's a lot of time spent talking, teaching, training, guiding, and keeping your children safe, with rare spankings, if you choose. They are not required. With two of our children, all you had to do was glance at them quickly, and they would fix their behavior. With one child, we spanked more than the other three combined. Now, our adopted daughter is twelve, and she was ten when she came to live with us. With her traumatic past, we do so much talking and occasionally grounding. Every child is different. Always finish talks and consequences with loving words filled with godly advice—*always!* Oh, and remember to ask questions and *listen*.

Here's an *important* side note: We have sat our older children down and apologized to them for some of our parenting failures and harsh punishments, which we did instead of loving discipline with counsel and instruction when they were younger. They understood our hearts were to be good parents and to do the best we could. It was a much-needed conversation that brought much-needed healing. Parents, don't be too proud to apologize when you get it wrong, even if it was twenty-five years ago. It's *not* too late. The relationship is more important than appearing or even being right. Adult children, do you know that most parents were really just trying to do the best they could? I'm not talking about abuse. I'm talking about parents who were really trying, and they grounded, paddled, scolded, or dragged you to church trying to train and direct. Do you need to forgive your parents who really tried to do their best? The relationship is more important than being right. I promise you that when they die, you will wish you had.

Another oddly controversial topic is schooling. Some express strong opinions about homeschooling, whereas others are adamant public school parents. Then you have a few who are all about private school. I was just talking with a young momma this week. She has three beautiful boys and has started homeschooling the oldest. She got a lot of grief and negative comments from friends and family. She is a high energy, well-educated momma who loves learning and is a great teacher. Out of five children, we have done all three schooling methods.

We loved our season of homeschooling. Please note that we had joint custody of our middle son, so during the school year, he resided with his mom during the week and with us every other weekend and most of the summer. He did not ever homeschool. Our eldest, after eleventh grade, attended ministry school for almost three years. Our youngest son graduated from private school, and our daughter and middle son graduated from public school. They all went on to college and are amazing adults. I regret not having my eldest son get an actual diploma, not just the one from the homeschool curriculum. It didn't hinder his attending Bible school or going into the military, but some other colleges required a diploma or GED.

This is a good topic to think about short term and long term, too. For example, maybe you will homeschool until a certain grade or you will send them to public school as long as it's safe or you will make sure they are getting music and art and PE in a private school. There are a lot of things to consider, but you need to decide what's best for you and your children. Consider making a diploma/GED the minimum, with your Momistry being to keep them safe: body, soul, and spirit. For us, our two sons did better in a private school. They are both big on justice and would have spent a lot of time confronting bullies and unjust teachers in a public school setting. They also do better in smaller classrooms. Our middle son never had an issue in public school, other than maybe being bored. Our older daughter was president of the debate team and made a huge impact on some other students. She actually performed the wedding ceremony for a couple of friends she met in high school. Currently with our twelve-year-old, we have done some homeschooling, as she was three years behind in school when she came to live with us. She has done public school and knew how to work the system and teachers, so we put her in a small private school to learn to manage classroom behaviors. Now, she is in a larger private school with smaller classes.

Listen, these are your children, and you can ebb and flow with their needs and your needs. I know a family where their children were all connected with friends who were a bad influence. The children were followers and could not hold to their personal convictions, so the parents pulled them out of public school and finished up their schooling online. I know another family where the children had worked so far ahead in their homeschool curriculum that they graduated at thirteen and fourteen and started doing virtual college classes. Don't panic. Decide with your spouse, and do tons of research. Homeschooling can be super fun, and public school might challenge them more academically, and private school may be easier for managing super social kiddos. What's important to you? After you decide, like we mentioned previously, write it down and revisit and change it as needed per child. You do YOU! Well, in this case, it's really doing what works best for the child.

Remember back in chapter 1 when I talked about talking through things with your spouse and agreeing ahead of time on how you might prefer to respond to something and writing it down? That is vital. Someone once called them presets, just like you set the dial on your car radio. You might say, "This is our family preset." Kids may want tattoos or piercings or to wear booty shorts or color or chop their hair. Also, there are topics to think about like depression, mental health issues, and cutting. There is a whole subculture of cutters. Think ahead, be preemptive, pray, talk, and write it down.

Our older daughter came to us when she was almost eighteen and asked about getting a tattoo. In Missouri, if you're under eighteen, you have to have a parent sign for you. She wanted a Scripture tattooed between her shoulder blades on her back. When she showed it to us, it was about the size of a business card. She felt strongly that the Scripture was one for her, and she had peace about it and had already been thinking about it for months. We asked if we could take a few days, then we got back together with her. We agreed that she could do what she felt led to do. I'm not saying that she said God told her to do it. I'm saying that the Holy Spirit did not tell her not to. Thus, she had peace. Ugh, okay, for those religious folks, choose your battles. Jesus has a tattoo on his thigh (see Revelation 19:16), and in Ezekiel 9:4, the foreheads of the intercessors were marked. If you want to argue the Leviticus 19 verse, I'd have to ask if you are following all of the commands in that chapter and the 613 other commands. Most of us are just over here trying to love and serve Jesus and not strain out a gnat. Let me get back to the story: So she and a girlfriend went to get tattoos. Afterward, she sent me a photo via text. What was originally 3.5 inches wide by 2 inches tall had ended up 11 inches wide and 7 inches tall and was bright red and swollen. Yes, I sat in my car in the driveway of our home and ugly cried. This was my baby girl. My text response was: "Oh, that's bigger than I expected. How are you feeling?" It was a good five or more years before I ever told her about my meltdown in the car. I put the ointment on that tattoo for her every night.

Her Scripture verse is: *"Where you go I will go, and where you stay I will stay. Your people will be my people and your God my God" (Ruth 1:16).*

This was well over a decade ago, and I have heard people ask her about her tattoo, and I've heard her talk to them about God and her commitment to always follow Him. One of those people was my dad, who is presently wrestling out his salvation. He was intrigued and had a lot of questions for her. Of course when she has traveled overseas, she was also able to talk to people. Mostly, it's been an anchor Scripture for her, as she's seen the good, the bad, and the ugly of church, people, and life. She will stay where God is, and she has. This is Momistry, keeping them safe: body, soul, and spirit. What will a tattoo matter in eternity?

On another note, my first favorite second daughter-in-love had gotten numerous tattoos as soon as she turned eighteen. She moved out of the nest quickly and was trying her wings. Now, six years later, she is paying to painfully have most of them removed. It was something that the Holy Spirit convicted her about, and she was obedient. Everyone's journey is different. As a parent, try saying, "Do you think that you will still want that tattooed on the top of your feet when you're fifty?"—instead of something like "Tattoos are sinful"—to your child. God is all about relationships, not religion, and we want to be safe, relationship-minded people for our children.

Tattoos are one topic that parents bring up to me occasionally. Our eldest son was in the military. After boot camp, he and a whole group of his battle buddies went and got tattoos together. This was not a drunken action of getting a tattoo of the name of some woman he just met. These were men who were warriors and committed to die for their country and for one another. Some of them did.

So here's a word that you never heard five years ago: cringy. If you heard it, it was in the context of a child doing a major wipeout on their bike or an Olympian crashing a bobsled or a toddler having a huge fall down some stairs, something that could've sent them to the hospital or heaven. It wasn't because so-and-so has formula bottles in their fridge or her kids are in public school or they eat fast food or that person got vaccinated. I literally saw a woman cringe when my nurse girlfriend and I were talking about both having gotten the COVID-19 vaccine. Her face grimaced, her eyes got huge, and she kind of did the nose up in the air thing. I mean, if I were twenty-four, it may have hurt my feelings. Imagine the pressure that kind of response puts on other women.

> **God is all about relationships, not religion, and we want to be safe, relationship-minded people for our children.**

One young mom said, "When you talk about depression, it triggers me." Another said, "When you post anti-vaccine posts, it triggers me." Yet another said, "When you testify about your healing from trauma, it really bothers me." The list goes on. Can we all just get over ourselves and our cringing, triggering, and bothering? Have you ever stopped and thought, "Why does this trigger me?" Have you thought, "Jesus, can You heal this area of my life, so I no longer react to it negatively?" My fifty-five-year-old opinion is if we stopped trying to control people with our feelings and instead worked on controlling and understanding our own feelings, we could really start stepping into intimate relationships and maturity. I don't know for sure if that will work, but I'm willing to try.

Here's a thought: Imagine the cringe factor you'd experience as a pre-cross disciple of Jesus. He told them to drink His blood (see John 6:53), take up a cross (see Matthew 16:24), and wash others' feet (see John 3-15). At one point, He took a whip to the people trading in the

Temple (see John 2:15). Could you imagine if afterward John said, "You know, Jesus, that really triggered my past when you talked about drinking your blood?" Imagine if Peter said, "Jesus, it really bothered me when you said we have

> **God is more concerned with the state of people's hearts than with the state of their feelings.**
> **—A.W. Tozer**

to wash other peoples' feet. That's way beneath me, and it's disgusting with all the dust and animal poop and trash on the streets." When you hear cringy nowadays, a more accurate word would probably be "judgy." Be free from cringing or the influence of cringers, and be free from triggers and constantly being bothered. BE FREE, and let other people be free. Where the Spirit of the Lord is there is FREEDOM!

In closing this chapter, I want to encourage you that most mistakes you make with your kiddos are forgivable. At times they won't even know it or remember it. They just want to spend time with you, and they're not expecting you to be perfect. If you and your spouse want to make eating healthy a priority, then by all means pack your little coolers for the church potlucks, and live your life. Maybe you are more of a foodie and love your pasta and meat (me too). Don't you worry about the gluten free people or the vegans. You do YOU! Some want a small house and are doing the whole minimalistic thing. Others are buying larger homes and spreading out and hosting family and guests. Some moms prefer disposable diapers and others are only cloth. Some prefer water bottles or only BPA-free containers. Maybe the pastor's wife is into all-natural clothing made by hand by women freed from slavery in India with sandals made by hand by impoverished children in Somalia, while you are purchasing clothing off the clearance rack at Wal-Mart made by who-knows-who in China. Do you wear makeup on your face, or is it all natural? To color your hair or not to color your hair? Do you use a crib or co-sleep? What about an electric car or gas car? Do your research. PRAY, PRAY, PRAY. Talk to your doctor. Ask your mentor for wise counsel. After that, here are your filters: Will it matter in eternity? Does it keep my family safe: body, soul, and spirit? Is God bothered by this? Is it sinful? Do I have peace? Our only concern should be to please God and operate powerfully in our Momistry. In turn, we let other mommas be free to do the same with no cringing or judging.

**Momming is the best job ever and the hardest job ever. YOU CAN DO IT!**

## Prayer:

*Thank You, God, for Your Holy Spirit Who gives me wisdom and guidance. Please help me to make the best choices for my family. Help me to not fall into the trap of fearing what other people will think or say. You have given me a Spirit of power and of love and a sound mind* (see 2 Timothy 1:7). *I trust You and Your ways. I need You, Lord, to lead me by Your perfect peace. Amen.*

## Practical points and questions:

1. When someone shares their opposing opinion on something, I will not be moved.
2. My family and I will prayerfully consider what's best for us and allow others the grace to do what's best for them.
3. Writing down our presets is powerful and necessary.
4. Have I been set in my opinions and choices?
5. How can I encourage someone today who is different from me?
6. What are the graces on my life? Help me, Holy Spirit, not to put expectations on others.

# Notes:

# CHAPTER 10

## HELP

**Humble people ask for help.**
**Joyce Meyer**

HELP! Well, we don't usually yell it at the top of our lungs, do we? It's more like sobbing in the shower, power-eating a bag of cookies or half a gallon of ice cream, maybe binge-watching Netflix, or even late-night retail therapy. These are just band-aids, mommas. What you need is four hours away from being a mom, wife, housekeeper, cook, nurse, and all the hats we wear as mommas. Maybe it looks like lunch with a friend, or maybe it's a massage or mani pedi—but regardless, it's with no kids, no husband, and no family unless your sister, cousin, or mom are your BFF. Send the hubby and kids to the park with lunch from McDonalds, then take a bath or a long, uninterrupted nap. You have to put your phone down *away* from your bed or bath. You can even grab a coffee and just go for a drive. Take some time, and just wander around Target or Costco for hours, though make sure to set a spending limit for yourself *before* arrival. How about calling a housekeeper? That's a good use of a tax refund or unexpected bonus. One time, I asked for a housecleaning for Mother's Day. ASK!

That's what the real battle is: It's asking. We think, or social media tells us, that we need to be some supermom, when in reality, we might feel ten steps behind where we want to be. We are late to everything, and the kids' clothes are clean, but they don't really match or aren't the right clothes for the day. This is a generation of kids who are comfortable with mismatched socks and slip-on and velcro shoes; it's faster. When we are always functioning in fourth gear and going a hundred MPH, it's difficult, if not impossible, to be present, and we are constantly exhausted. God never intended for you to burn yourself out parenting. You are His daughter, and He wants you to take care of you. The moment we realize that how we react to our kids has more to do with *how we're feeling* than what our child is doing is the moment we understand the importance, as moms, of keeping ourselves emotionally healthy.

Consider your family unit as a team, so you can implement teamwork. Everyone in the house works together for success, not perfection. Ah, I'm going to call this one out right here. Your house is not meant to be perfect; it's meant to be an excellent place full of safety and peace (aka organized chaos). Be free from the spirit of perfectionism. It's oppressive and a taskmaster.

> **The moment we realize that how we react to our kids has more to do with *how we're feeling* than what our child is doing is the moment we understand the importance, as moms, of keeping ourselves emotionally healthy**

The only perfect person, ever, is Jesus. *"But since you excel in everything—in faith, in speech, in knowledge, in complete earnestness and in love…" (2 Corinthians 8:7a)* Excellence is the goal, not perfection.

A few years back, an old neighbor friend invited our children and I over for lunch and a playdate one afternoon. Her home was always immaculate, and the food she served was delightful. The snacks for the children were homemade, each of them having their own personally labeled cup for freshly squeezed lemonade. She and her husband had three children who were close to the same age as my four children at the time. The kids were all playing in her backyard while she and I enjoyed time chatting and visiting. Our husbands were both at work. She shared with me how she was weary and wanted to just run away and had looked at flights to the state where her extended family lived, flights only for herself. I was shocked, as she'd always seemed to have everything together. She started to cry and unloaded years of perfectionistic performance to me. I held her hand and listened attentively while she cried. This was a mountain that I had already climbed. After my neighbor friend finished crying and we talked about the flight mode that she was in, I shared with her my story of battling perfectionism and about the vicious trap it is. She immediately confessed to struggling with this her whole life. I used the same quote as my mentor from years before: "There is no such thing as a perfect family. We work towards excellence and doing our best."

I got my phone out and opened the Bible app and read her the verse from 1 Corinthians 10. I was beaming, expecting her to have the same epiphany that I had experienced. Instead, she just stared at me blankly, so I changed tactics to discuss her to-do list. How many of you moms have to-do lists? I'm a list-maker and love checking things off, but my lists are quite a bit shorter these days. We spent over an hour trying to delegate some of the tasks. Her children were twelve, eight, and five. They were old enough to be helping with some of the list, and her husband could of course help as well. She refused to let go of any of her to-do lists, because she said they wouldn't do it right. Coming to terms with the fact that my way was not the only way to do things was major for me in letting go. (This is where all the moms burst out in the "Let It Go" song from Frozen.) Doing your best and using excellence is the best way to live.

One night, our youngest son had a friend over. As was custom in our home, they took their shoes off as they came in. While they were playing video games, I was sitting on the couch behind them and noticed my son's friend, an only child, had bright white, perfectly matching socks. My son's socks were dingy and were two totally different brands. I laughed to myself, realizing that I had been set free from perfectionism. We went from nicely folded socks in perfectly organized dresser drawers to a sock basket, and everyone would find what they needed. My daughter preferred to pull her socks out and match them; however, they usually ended up on top of her dresser and not in the drawer. Now, don't judge me. Everyone had clean socks, and nice church socks were folded when they came out of the dryer, but this was no longer a battle for me. About a year after our youngest son got married, I carried that sock basket right out to the dumpster. I may or may not have done a little dance and given a little shout of FREEDOM.

I get it: Society was easier fifty years ago when grandmas and grandpas were helping and commonly even living in the home, and in some cultures that's still the case today. Take a minute, and breathe a few deep, slow breaths, then look for areas where you need help. Get a piece of paper and write down four people you know will help you. It can be your mom or MIL (mother-in-law), sister, cousin, friend, neighbor, daycare provider, aunt, or a Mom's Day Out program. I know a few grandma ladies at our church (I am one of them) who are willing to help with kiddos on occasion. All you have to do is ask! What are some areas you could use some help?

<u>Cooking:</u> Shop pre-made meals. Use the Crockpot and Instant Pot, and make large amounts for easy leftovers. Sign up for coupons for buy one get one or 50% off or earn pizza points. Ask friends what they do. Ask a friend to come and meal prep with you. I double up when cooking to have leftovers or freeze some for a quick meal on a night when I neglect to plan. If you're not on a strict budget, try DoorDash or UberEats. Don't beat yourself up if once a month it's cereal for dinner

with a movie so you can take a hot bath, or it's grilled cheese and ramen. Unless your family has some special dietary needs (not wants), this is an area in which you can lighten up pretty easily. Also, it's okay to ask your mom or MIL to make you some of her famous chicken and dumplings.

The first time I met my future MIL was at a Thanksgiving meal at my house. I was raised in California, and she was raised in the south. The turkey had just come out of the oven and was resting, and my MIL came into the kitchen just as I was pulling out a pan for gravy. She picked up a jar and asked graciously, "What is this?" I replied, "It's gravy." She was quiet for a minute and then very kindly asked if she could make homemade gravy. Of course I allowed her to. She also made homemade noodles with my four-year-old daughter the next day, with a rolling pin and everything. Don't be too prideful to ask for or allow someone to help you. Twenty-five years later, after training from my MIL, I am now a pretty good gravy maker.

<u>Housework:</u> Have you tried a chore list for everyone in the house? Also, if you're a new mommy, get the toddlers helping you early. Two-year-olds can put silverware away or wipe off the table (poorly) or dust end tables. A five-year-old can unload the dishwasher, fold towels, rinse plates and cups, clean and set the table, dust, or vacuum (if your vacuum is not too heavy or if he or she is not afraid of it). Our kids called our old Kirby "Jaws," and it weighed well over thirty pounds. My twelve-year-old loves to steam mop. Every child is different, so they may like something and hate something else. Their future spouses will thank you for this training too.

When they are young, it is a great time to train them to be part of the team. Two- or three-year-olds want to help mommy and daddy usually. Fold towels with them. Have them show grandma the towels they folded or the end table they dusted. My almost three-year-old granddaughter likes to help her daddy with yard work. She picks up toys and puts them away, helps her mommy with dishes, and likes to vacuum with the handheld. My two-year-old grandson helps his daddy shovel the snow from the driveway and helps him with yard work. He also picks up toys and puts them away, and he likes to sweep, especially the deck. Oh, he likes to play with my Roomba too, but that doesn't count. My twelve-year-old daughter unloads the dishwasher, makes her own packed school lunch each night for the next day (as we are not morning people), and does all of her own laundry. She helps me with vacuuming some, and she shoveled snow a few weekends back (although it was only for 10 minutes). The day before yesterday, she peeled and chopped cucumbers for the salad.

There are instructions for plenty of chore lists on Pinterest you can make. Amazon has some for sale. You can even use a dry erase board or a piece of paper. We have assigned chores before, rotated chores, and let them pick and trade. We are never demanding about chores, and we encourage teamwork. It's all about teamwork; however, I have been known to get a fourteen-year-old out of bed because he or she didn't unload the dishwasher (their chore of choice for the week), which needed to be done so I could wash the dishes in the sink. That's love and logic or tough love, or something like that.

<u>Laundry:</u> It helped me to throw a load in before I went to bed and put it in the dryer in the morning. Train at home age-appropriate children to fold clothes, or sheesh, it's really okay to leave it in the basket for a few days. BE FREE. At the moment of me typing this paragraph, there's a load of towels on the chair in my lanai. Hopefully my husband will walk by and get it. We will see. I used to have three laundry baskets:

one for clothes that need to be washed, one for clothes that need to be folded, and one for clothes that need to be put away. By ten years old, our kiddos could do their own laundry. If it has a hole in it, it goes in the trash or to Goodwill, unless it's an expensive piece. If it's a dress or a suit coat, we use a seamstress who is priced super reasonably. (I don't sew. I can, but it's tedious and exasperating for me and not worth my time.) Thrift stores are handy if we need cheap clothes. Also, hand-me-downs are absolutely acceptable. In high school and sometimes middle school, clothes can become a bigger deal. Clean, free of most holes and stains, and proper fit: Those were my goals. For school shopping, I gave them a dollar amount. If they wanted a name brand, the dollars were not going to go very far. We start talking about this in July, so there is plenty of time to mow or sweep the garage or clean out a cabinet or drawer or pull weeds, etc. to earn some shopping money. We are not doing them any favors by giving them every name brand thing we did not have; that creates entitlement. We are training future adults here. Some will be world changers, doctors, presidents, pastors, counselors, and most importantly, *moms and dads.*

<u>Grocery Shopping:</u> One positive thing that came with the COVID-19 pandemic was grocery pick up and Instacart. Target also has same-day pick up. I've gone there at 8PM in my jammies. Oh, and I've purchased a gift or two with the gift bag on the Target app. They brought it to my car, and I quickly put it together. At Christmas, I did some Black Friday shopping this way as well and got the sale price too. Our local grocery store has a drive up with orders over $35, which is an easy limit to hit. My eldest daughter used to go grocery shopping every Sunday. It was a ritual for her and her husband. When they had one child, that was totally doable. Now, they have a two-year-old and a four-

month-old, and she sings the highest praises of Aldi grocery pick up. My youngest son and his wife use Instacart, as they both work full time and are youth leaders and help with the worship team at our church. Our other two sons are DoorDash kings. I think they have an app and everything. I'm kind of all over the place with these tools, but I'm so grateful for the time and energy they save. Personally, I think I save $15 a month with Instacart by not impulse buying items.

<u>Work</u>: Not all mommas in the Momistry are SAHMs. Some work or worked for a while. When working, I always had to tell my employer my family came first. Most places understood that, especially when my husband was deployed with the military. Make sure to set the boundary early, so they know what to expect. If you're planning to have a child next year, tell your boss. They can help facilitate your maternity leave or move you to a remote position or plan for your transition to leave permanently while training your replacement. Remember, when you're in the Momistry, keeping your children safe,—body, soul, and spirit—is number one.

Your children can totally thrive at daycare. They can excel while staying with your mother-in-law or mom. As a grandma, this is my favorite. If getting a nanny is more your thing, do it. The purpose that God has for you is not the same one He has for anyone else, so you cannot compare. One of my dear friends at church is a very successful lawyer, and she has raised a brilliant daughter who is literally changing the world. My other friend is a nurse, and another a teacher. My favorite first daughter-in-love is a genius computer guru. You do you. Comparison is a robber. *"Oh, don't worry; we wouldn't dare say that we are as wonderful as these other men who tell you how important they are! But they are only comparing themselves with each other, using themselves as the standard of measurement. How ignorant!" (2 Corinthians 10:12)*

Mental Health: I know we talked about this in previous chapters, but I cannot express to you enough how much you need to get help if you're struggling in the area of mental health. Yes, pray. Yes, talk to a pastor. Yes, see a therapist, and yes, take meds for a season if needed. We don't set up a tent and camp out during hard seasons; we get help so we can walk through them. The sooner you get help, the sooner the rough season is in the rear-view mirror. It's okay not to be okay.

In my fifty-six years, I've never heard a mom say "Wow, this is so easy" about parenting. As you've heard me say, "Momming is the best job ever and the hardest job ever. YOU CAN DO IT!" You're not alone in this. We all cry. We all lose it sometimes. We all yell at a child or forget an event or whatever. We all need help. Find a tribe at a church or friends or family or neighbors. Hold on tightly to them.

> **We don't set up a tent and camp out during hard seasons; we get help so we can walk through them.**

When needed, ask them for help. Remember that paper you wrote down earlier in this chapter—those peeps. When they need help, be there for them. I have no idea where I'd be without my tribe.

If you don't have a tribe, you may have isolated yourself, or maybe you've relocated somewhere new recently. I'm going to assume you're reading this book because you're a believer in Jesus. In that case, momma, find yourself a church with young people. Connect with a mom's group on Facebook from your area. Use Google to find Mother's Day Out programs. Connection can be hard, if not impossible, if you don't initiate. There is a group that will knock on your door and talk about Jesus. Beware, they will make you give up coffee, so if you want a group of latte mommas with colored hair, jewelry, and makeup, find yourself a local church by knocking on the doors yourself.

**Momming is the best job ever and the hardest job ever. YOU CAN DO IT!**

## Prayer:

*I come against pride right now in the name of Jesus. Sometimes I need help, and I will start asking for it. God, please give me wisdom and discernment in areas that are overwhelming me. Help me to be patient with my spouse, children, and myself as we do hard things together. I'm thankful for my tribe, and boy do I need them. Guide and counsel me with Your Holy Spirit to not do Momistry alone or isolate myself. Amen.*

## Practical points and questions:

1. What area or areas do you need to ask for help in?
2. Who are people in your tribe you can ask for help?
3. Do you have a mom, MIL, or mother figure you can ask to cook you a meal or give you some pointers on managing meals?
4. Are you struggling to ask for help? Why?
5. If you're working, have you set a "family first" boundary with your employer?

## Notes:

# CHAPTER 11

## Then They're Grown

> **Remember, the goal is not to raise great kids; it's to raise kids who become great adults.**
>
> **Andy Andrews**

In this season of my life, I get to watch my grandbabies quite often. For my daughter, I get to spend time with her son, who is two, every Wednesday and her daughter, who is nine months old, every Thursday. On occasion I get to hang out with my oldest grandbaby, Maelee. She's three and in preschool. A few weeks back, on a Thursday, my dear friend came over, and we had Panera deliver lunch while we visited. She enjoyed getting to hold and feed the baby. While we were talking, she said, "I feel like parenting adult children is much harder than parenting babies or toddlers." After thinking on that for several weeks, I thought that maybe adding this chapter could help those of us in that season of life, or help those who are getting close to it to prepare for that part of your journey.

Personally, I feel like the reason it's hard to parent adult children is because they can so quickly cut you out of their life. Looking back, I'm glad we had so many talks with our children about honor and what God says about honoring your parents. As adults they no longer need to obey their parents, but they are commanded to honor them. I mean, it's a big deal when God puts it in His top ten commandments. God has blessed me with close relationships with all of my adult children, including the ones I didn't birth.

One time, an elderly relative said to me, "You have to watch how you treat your daughters-in-law, because they can keep you from seeing your son and grandchildren." That kind of shocked me. My plan was to always treat them with love, respect, and kindness, as I try to do towards most people. I also planned to, and have, apologized when I've overstepped my bounds or maybe said something uncomfortable or inappropriate. I'm probably biased, but I think I have the most amazing son-in-love and daughters-in-love in the universe. God picked the perfect spouses for my children. When my sons and daughter married, they were to "leave and cleave." *"This explains why a man leaves his father and mother and is joined to his wife, and the two are united into one."* (*Genesis 2:24*)

I never fully understood it when parents said, "I can't wait for them to turn eighteen and move out." Two of our children lived at home until marriage. They stayed under our covering and provision, working and saving, saving, saving. We all text at least weekly but most of us daily. We have a family group text for quick updates and funny memes. I respect each one of them as adults and men and women of God. They are His sons and daughters. We have had miscommunications and times when hurtful "jokes" were said, but regardless, keeping the connection and relationship was vital. God is all about family.

If you are longing for reconciliation with your child or children, don't give up hope. There are several mommas my age and older with whom God is restoring their relationships with their adult children. Listen to the Holy Spirit. Choose humility.

> **Modeling humility doesn't diminish your authority.**
> **—Lisa Bevere**

Remember that the relationship is much more important than being right. Lisa Bevere says, "Modeling humility doesn't diminish your authority." I still apologize to my children. I can make a flippant remark about something that sounds snarky. The Holy Spirit will nudge me about it, so I quickly call or text or go over to them and apologize. Regardless of the age of your estranged child, do not give up hope. *"For God was in Christ, reconciling the world to himself, no longer counting people's sins against them. And he gave us this wonderful message of reconciliation." (2 Corinthians 5:19)* Hold on tight to the message of reconciliation and pray, pray, pray. <u>Nothing</u> is impossible for God.

My eldest son and favorite first daughter-in-love graciously open their home for a family meal almost every Thursday night. We occasionally switch hosting to give them a break, but it's rare. Their home is perfect to host all of us, and, well, my daughter-in-love is a closet chef. She spoils us, literally. They also love hosting people. Anyway, several weeks back, on one of those Thursday nights, the kids all started poking fun at me as we were leaving. It got to be a bit intense, and my feelings were hurt. It took me a good day to process this, which I was scolded for, because we always had immediate knee-to-knee family meetings when the children were growing up. I finally asked the two adult children involved if we could meet, and we did (via Zoom, but it worked). I was able to express my feelings, and they were able to apologize and explain that they were joking. They were also able to share their feelings, and I was quick to apologize for being dramatic.

There was a season, when my children were just becoming adults, that their dad/stepdad and I sat down with them to apologize. We went through a lot of ups and downs in their years growing up. Between divorce court, military moves, moves from financial crisis, religious extremism, and following misguided teachings, we had blundered through so much. We were so busy fighting to give them a good God kind of life that we missed it, often. Each child was immediately forgiving. Thankfully, they had the wisdom to see where their lives could have been had we just stuck with the way we were raised or with family patterns. They knew that our hearts were to give each of them a much better life. We did not do it perfectly, but they are all thriving, independent, successful adults who love God and love each other. That old saying "Let our ceiling be their floor" was always our heart.

> **A mother's job is to teach her children to not need her anymore. The difficult part of that job is accepting that they don't need her anymore.**

You don't hear much talk of the season in life where you are juggling ailing parents, still parenting a twelve-year-old, and also have adult children with babies. This is where learning years ago from Pastor Diana, my mentor, how to honor my parents has been so important. My mom passed away about five years ago. During her last seven to ten years of life, she was in and out of the hospital. Her last six months were spent in hospice where we all were allowed to spend a lot of time with her. My dad, who is still alive and lives 1500 miles away, is maybe having some onset of dementia. He struggles with forgetting words and life events, being moody and isolating himself, and some balance and depth perception issues, and he sometimes struggles to learn new things, although I'm super proud of him for upgrading his television to a smart TV. I still try to communicate with him weekly. We, my kids included, have all encouraged him to move here, but he has some lame excuse about the warm California weather in comparison to Missouri's all four seasons (and sometimes bitter days in the winter). Regardless of how he is feeling or behaving, I still strive to treat him with the honor he is due. At the same time, I'm changing diapers and chasing a two-year-old and helping with seventh grade social studies homework. I think this might be why my girlfriend made that comment about parenting adult children being more difficult. When your parents get into their senior years, you can kind of become their parent. There are the eighty-year-olds who are declining and the thirty-year-olds who are in their prime, then you're fifty-six in the middle somewhere. It's a wonderful, yet difficult season.

Sidenote about menopause and perimenopause: Listen ladies, this is the real deal. Maybe your family talked about it, but mine did not. After birthing my youngest child, I had my tubes tied. Subsequently, I went off birth control pills. Within five or six years, my periods started to become sporadic, and when they did come, I found myself looking for maxi maxi pads or super maxi tampons at the store (which they don't make, by the way). I'd also started waking up at night super hot and would have occasional moments of hot flashes throughout the day. One Sunday at church, I had gone through two maxi pads in an hour and had even spotted on my pants. As I came out of the bathroom, I walked up to a group of my friends to see if any of them had any pads or tampons and to ask if my pants spot was visible (it was not). I commented on some of my crazy cycles and extreme bleeding. Two of the four ladies asked if I'd had my hormones checked for perimenopause. I thought to myself, "What? I'm thirty-seven. That happens to old ladies." I got a quick church foyer infomercial from my friends on perimenopause. The next day, I called my doctor. Apparently hormones were only checked when requested, and I had to pay for the testing out of pocket, which I hope changes with doctors and insurance companies as time goes on. I got the test done and paid the lab. Yep, my hormones were low, and I was perimenopausal. First, the doctor put me on a low-dose birth control pill, and that helped manage the cycles and ebb the hot flashes.

After about five years, my periods stopped altogether. That's when they call it menopause, so we stopped the birth control pill. Yeah, that was a crazy train for almost a year: exhaustion, moodiness, hot flashes, night sweats, anxiety, insomnia, and weight gain. Every orifice was dry, my hair was falling out, and my libido was zilch. I went back to my same group of friends, and they told me about hormone replacement therapy. I'm not sure why my doctor didn't recommend this, so I immediately connected with an HRT (hormone replacement therapy) doctor and set up a screening. They did more lab work that I had to pay for out of pocket, and she came up with a plan and submitted it to my primary care doctor. Yep, over ten years later, I'm still on HRT. My life is much too busy to spend it on that crazy train. Now, don't let this cause fear. I have a friend who never had one menopausal symptom. Her periods simply stopped. God can do miracles! For me, He used my friends and doctors.

My daughter and I talk daily. She's one of my closest friends now. She was not my friend when she was a child or teen. I guess when she was in her early twenties, still living at home, we started to become more like friends. After she married and moved out, we became great friends. I remember the first Christmas after she moved out. She married in November, so it was soon after. I started to wrap presents and sat on the floor with all of the paper and bows and tape and tags and ribbon and such. After I started to wrap the first gift, I just began to cry—ugly cry. All of a sudden, I realized that she and I had wrapped gifts together for almost twenty years. She is such a better gift wrapper than I am. She color coordinates and gets the creases straight and makes fancy ribbons.

We would always talk and have hot cocoa with coconut creamer (it's a game changer—try it) and snacks. We cranked up the cassette player with Chipmunks Christmas when she was younger and the CD player with Michael Buble on repeat when she was older. During that first year, there were no drinks, snacks, music, or fancy packages for Christmas wrapping. I got blindsided by a tradition that I didn't know was a thing.

The next year at Christmas, I downloaded a Pentatonix Christmas album and Trans-Siberian Orchestra with King and Country's "Drummer Boy" onto my Apple Music and cranked it up on my Google Home. I made myself some decaf coffee with peppermint mocha creamer and grabbed a few cookies for a snack. I'd gone to Hobby Lobby where they are so considerate to have all of the matching things sold together, so I loaded up on paper and bows and tags and ribbon. At my age, I moved to the table instead of the floor. I still miss wrapping presents with one of my best friends, but I'm enjoying the table and chair with a cushion and back support. It's difficult. I could ask her, and she would come over, but do you know what? It's time for her to make traditions with her little family in her Momistry.

We never stop protecting our children, even when they're in their thirties. I've had to kindly and graciously ask an adult child about their unhealthy weight, another for working too much, another for not **Momistry is protecting their bodies, souls, and spirits, and that doesn't stop when they move out. Well, it shouldn't.** caring for themselves, another for being harsh with their spouse. I approached one when he/shee was struggling with depression, offered financial help to another, and confronted one when they were just being a jerk because they were overwhelmed in life. I usually don't say anything as training. I've already done that when they were little. If I see them in a difficult spot, I ask them questions and give advice only *if* asked. Sometimes they just want to vent to Mom, or as my youngest son says, "Mom, I just need you to hold the bucket while I verbally vomit." Now, that's not free reign for him to speak out against others. He's an adult, so it's usually just me listening as he talks through a problem and solves it on his own. There were times I'd pick him up from middle school, and he would verbally vomit all over the car about all of the tween drama going on, after which we would problem solve together or just LET IT GO (usually the best advice for drama)! Momistry is protecting their bodies, souls, and spirits, and that doesn't stop when they move out. Well, it shouldn't.

## Momming is the best job ever and the hardest job ever, and being a grandma is AWESOME. YOU CAN DO IT!

## Prayer:

*God, thank You for every season of life. Thank You for always being with me and never leaving me. Your strength is shown in my weakness. Please give me wisdom during this season of life. There is so much to balance. Help me to always be honorable to my parents and to be available to my children and grandchildren. Your ways are higher than mine, and I fully embrace Your ways. God, You have only been good to me. I am overwhelmed with Your goodness and mercy. You treat me so much better than I deserve. Amen.*

## Practical points and questions:

1. Are you showing honor to your parents and your in-laws?
2. How are your hormones? Do you have a doctor who talks with you about every season of life?
3. Do you need to humble yourself and apologize to your children for any past poor parenting?
4. If you're not yet a grandma, start dreaming about it. What fun adventures do you want to go on with your grandbabies?

# Notes:

# CHAPTER 12

## Welcome to Your Momistry

> This is my command—be strong and courageous! Do not be afraid or discouraged. For the Lord your God is with you wherever you go.
>
> **Joshua 1:9**

Welcome to your Momistry! You are committed to the work or vocation of dedicating your life to the ministry of raising children who love God and love family. Your mission is to keep children in your care safe: body, soul, and spirit. It is a world-changing ministry. Take a minute and congratulate yourself for taking the charge of Momistry seriously and for finishing this book. With the amount of busyness everyone is in the midst of, making time to read can be a challenge. Whether it's this book or some of the books I've mentioned in the resources, you won't ever regret time invested into training for you and your family. We should all be in a constant state of learning and growing.

With the emphasis in this book on keeping our children safe, becoming a momma bear is so important. We have to be

> When you stop growing you start dying.
> —**William S. Burroughs**

willing to do some very hard things sometimes, but we don't do it alone. *"This is my command—be strong and courageous! Do not be afraid or discouraged. For <u>the Lord your God is with you wherever you go</u>." (Joshua 1:9, emphasis mine)* Even just last week I had to drop everything and run to the school to help with some tween drama. I also had a parent-teacher conference last week and have another tomorrow. I initiated the conferences to make sure education and excellence were kept at our agreed-upon standard. That's my child's soul, safety, learning accountability, and responsibility: Hard stuff right there. I had to walk away from my lunch and a business meeting to go deal with the drama. There hasn't been much immediate fruit from any of it this week, but I know there will be in the years to come. Be free to be a momma bear, and be empowered by the Holy Spirit to do the hard things. YOU CAN DO IT!

Yesterday, I was helping with a meet and greet event at church and heard one of my pastors talking to a young couple about the importance of mentorship. Were you able to connect with someone in your circle to mentor you? The only way to really change what we are currently doing is by receiving new tools from others. The accountability factor is super impactful as well. It is helpful to read books and follow some other strong Momistry-minded mommas, but there is so much more to be said about having lunch with someone, prayer, and a hug—a huge, awkwardly-long hug. No one likes being held accountable, yet it is priceless in helping us change as a mom, wife, friend, or whatever. We need each other, and I sure need wiser women speaking into my life; however, at fifty-six years old, I find myself to be the oldest woman in the room way too often lately. Have you seen that meme that says something like, "I was looking to see who the adult was in the room and realized it was me"? At my age, that's a real thing.

> **For God has not given us a spirit of fear and timidity, but of power, love, and self-discipline.**
> **—2 Timothy 1:7**

The biggest discussion surrounding children that I hear almost everywhere I go is the topic of sex, pornography, gender issues, and lust. Don't wait to start teaching your children about these topics and what

God says about them; initiate age-appropriate discussion at every level. I share some helpful books in the resources, and there are some great podcasts out there too. Most importantly, you want them to be comfortable talking to you about anything and everything. You want to be their safe person, so don't freak out if your six-year-old boy draws a penis and testicles (balls) on his Thanksgiving turkey art project that he made in his kindergarten classroom. His turkey was Tom, a male, and that is anatomically correct for a human. Maybe explain that male turkeys have a cloaca, which is a good science lesson. Now, if your seventh grader (or older) is drawing sexual parts in art class, you might need to step up the dialogue. This is about talking and discussing and asking questions and training, not lecturing. The enemy wants to pervert it and make it shameful and dirty. Sex is a beautiful gift that God has given to married couples to unwrap. Keep it wrapped, kiddos.

Speaking of marriage, how's being married with children going for you? Are you making sure to stay united with your spouse? Date nights and time just as spouses are so vital. Yesterday, my tween daughter began to tell her dad something by saying, "Don't tell Mom, but I…" My husband immediately responded with, "Sweetie, Mom and I are on the same team. I don't keep secrets from her." Dad had to immediately investigate the shenanigans and make sure that proper action took place. The enemy might try to use our children to put a wedge in our marriage, and we must be vigilant not to allow that to happen. Remember that your spouse is your forever relationship; kids grow up and move out. How about you single mommas? Are you walking out forgiveness of your ex-husband or baby daddy? I know it's difficult, but YOU CAN DO IT!

Learning about generational patterns and behaviors was such a game changer for me. Once I met Jesus, I knew 110% that I wanted a different life for my children, and I finally had hope for that. It took years to walk out, but knowing that I didn't want to replicate my parents helped me be intentional in some areas that I had to battle to be free in. There were some lions, bears, and giants that had to be conquered. Have you taken the time to identify patterns in your family line? The Holy Spirit is so powerful to help us break those patterns by the blood of our Jesus. We get to start new patterns, strong and healthy (not perfect) ones, while keeping our children safe and raising them to love God and love family. It's hard work. YOU CAN DO IT!

In this season of life, the year 2022, the rate of inflation in the United States is higher than it has been in thirty years, so the high price of parenting just got higher. A sweatshirt I purchased for $24 dollars last year is $40 this year. Stick with a plan with your spouse on what's needed and what's wanted, and don't feel guilty. On the contrary, feel empowered to tell your money what to do. Financial disagreements are rated as the number one cause of divorce, so expose that plot of the enemy, and keep your family plan right in front of you. A good way to gauge is by asking yourself: "Is it an investment into my child's body, soul, or spirit?" Yes, pay for the summer Bible camp. Music is good, and sports are great for team training and discipline. Help them raise money for the homeless or children who are less fortunate than they are. A season of therapy might be needed for them to gain coping skills. Maybe a robotics class or coding training would be good. Keep it to a few activities so as not to overwhelm everyone, but invest, invest, invest. When you see your adult child run a marathon, play on the worship team, have a well-paying job in computers, or use their leadership and communication skills from debate to propel them into entrepreneurship, you will be amazed. My adult children are still amazing to me, especially as I watch some of them parent. Mommas, when you hold those grandbabies, it will be 110% worth every cent and second of your effort, I promise. Yes, it is better than you think.

Today I was texting with a young momma who recently had to sit down with her husband and redo their family planner and boundaries. They have four children ages six months to seven years, so their household is super busy. With kids going in different directions and church and extended family and hubby's job being demanding, they needed to dial things down a few notches. They enlisted grocery store pick up and delegated some chores to the older kiddos. Each spouse talked to their extended family and limited attendance at some parties and family gatherings. When we were texting, it had been a few months since they implemented these new boundaries, and she said, "I feel the peace of God in my home again, and I'm not exhausted."

Like my friend had to do in the last paragraph, sometimes you have to sit down with your spouse and discuss where you are on your journey. Hers was: "Mom needs some help, y'all."

> **Burnout isn't caused by being too busy, it's caused by not setting healthy boundaries.**
> —Dr. Caroline Leaf

Life is full of choices: schooling, home ownership, career goals, vaccinations, churches, pets, breast feeding, and so on. Learn to ebb and flow with it. Always do what's best for you and your family. Do whatever is in line with your Momistry of keeping everyone safe: body, soul, and spirit. My eldest daughter likes to say: "Don't get caught up in the weeds of it." That's such a healthy way to look at things. Remember, don't compare, and take your time. Also, always be led by the peace of God. If you crash on the curb of life, just turn the wheel and get back on the road. Make sure you choose the narrow path (see Matthew 7:13-14).

Momming is the best job ever and the hardest job ever. YOU CAN DO IT! You're probably tired of hearing me say that by now, but it's not a cliche. It is absolutely 100% the truth. It's a hard job, and sometimes we need help, and that's okay. BE FREE! No one, and I mean no one, expects you to parent on your own. Did you find your tribe? If you have set boundaries, made choices that suit your family, and are still struggling, get some help from your tribe, or at least tell your spouse, mom, or best friend. Sometimes it helps to just say it outloud and have a good cry. Well, that's helped me, anyway. Your Momistry is too important. Your kiddos need you at 100% so you can keep them safe: body, soul, and spirit. It's okay to ask for help. Just do it.

If you're in the season of grown children, don't quit your Momistry. If you're enjoying this time of empty nesting while waiting for your Grandmomistry, remember that there are young mommas in need of spiritual mentors. Put yourself out there. Maybe your relationship with your grown children is estranged. If so, pray, pray, pray and hold tight to the promise of reconciliation. Regardless of who your parents are, you are commanded to honor them (see Exodus 20:12). I know it's hard when they get older and cranky. Celebrate this season. You may be a menopausal mess, but do you know what? The best is *only* getting better!

# Momming is the best job ever and the hardest job ever, and being a grandma is AWESOME. YOU CAN DO IT!

Take a few deep breaths, grab hold of the Holy Spirit, and feel empowered to step into your Momistry. You are a vital part of the advancement of the Kingdom of God. Keep filling your toolbelt and growing, then remember to share tools with friends, family, and anyone trying to raise children who love God and love family. Now that you've finished this book, jump onto Facebook and find the group Her Entourage. It is a private group for moms, moms-to-be, future moms, foster moms, stepmoms, guardians, and even a few of us grandmas. This will be a safe place where we can pray for each other and share tools and encourage one another. Consider it to be your entourage of ladies.

## Prayer:

My Prayer for YOU: *Father God, I pray for my friends, my sisters, that You would empower them to fulfill their Momistry, their most important ministry. God, You have knit each of their children together especially for them. Give them wisdom to train them in Your ways, so they can be successful in the plans and purpose that You have created for them. I ask that You keep their children safe: body, soul, and spirit. Your blood, Jesus, is the most powerful covering for our children and our families. May they all be surrounded by Your presence and led only by Your peace and Your voice. Let each momma feel like she is a part of a vast community of women raising the future generations to love God and love their families. I thank You in advance. You are a good, good Father. Amen and Amen.*

## Notes:

# RESOURCES

*(All titles are books unless otherwise noted.)*

## Christian Women
Lisa Bevere
- Without Rival
- Lioness Arising
- Out Of Control And Loving It

Havilah Cunnington
- Leap into Love
- Stronger than the Struggle

Joyce Meyer
- Battlefield of the Mind
- Living Beyond Your Feelings

Podcasts
- setapartgirl, Leslie Ludy
- That Sounds Fun, Annie Downs
- Living Proof, Beth Moore
- Home with Havilah, Havilah Cunnington
- The Christine Caine Equip and Empower, Christine Caine

- Made For This, Jennie Allen
- WHOA That's Good, Sadie Robertson
- Conversations with John & Lisa Bevere, John & Lisa Bevere

Tools

- MessengerX, discipleship app from John and Lisa Bevere (https://messengerx.com/)

## Parenting

Dr. James Dobson
- Bringing Up Boys
- Bringing Up Girls

Danny Silk
- Loving Our Kids on Purpose

Gary Chapman
- 5 Love Languages Of Children

Stormie Omartian
- The Power of a Praying Parent

Dr. Karyn Purvis
- The Connected Parent

Podcasts
- Don't Mom Alone, Heather MacFadyen
- Risen Motherhood, Emily Jensen & Laura Wifler
- Busy Mom, Heidi St. John

- Pardon the Mess with Cynthia Yanof, Cynthia Yanof
- Courageous Parenting, Isaac & Angie Tolpin
- Focus on Parenting Podcast, Focus on the Family
- Calm Christian Parenting, Kirk Martin

**Mentorship**
Lisa Bevere
- Godmothers

Melissa Kruger
- Growing Together

Podcasts
- Face To Face Mentoring, Jayme Hull
- Productivity & Proverbs 31, Kathy Lanham

**Talking to Children about Sexuality**
Stan and Brenna Jones (God's Design for Sex series)
- The Story of Me (ages 3-5)
- What's the Big Deal (ages 8-12)
- Facing the Facts (ages 11-14)

Carolyn Nystrom
- Before I Was Born (ages 5-8)

Lisa Bevere
- Kissed the Girls and Made Them Cry

Zack and Kimberly King
- I Said No!

Kristen A. Jenson
- Good Pictures Bad Pictures

Tools
- bark, parental control app for keeping them safe on electronics (https://www.bark.us/)
- mSpy, parental control software for keeping them safe on electronics (https://www.mspy.com/)

## Marriage
Jimmy Evans
- Marriage on the Rock
- The Four Laws of Love
- Vision Retreat Guidebook

Kevin Leman
- Sheet Music

Danny Silk
- Keep Your Love On

Gary Chapman
- The 5 Love Languages

Dr. Emerson Eggerichs
- Love and Respect

Stormie Omartian
- The Power of a Praying Wife
- The Power of a Praying Husband

Dave & Ashley Willis
- The Naked Marriage

Craig & Amy Groeschel
- From This Day Forward

Podcasts
- Fierce Marriage, Ryan & Selena Frederick
- The Naked Marriage with Dave & Ashley Willis, Dave & Ashley Willis
- MarriageToday with Jimmy & Karen Evans, Jimmy & Karen Evans
- Focus on Marriage Podcast, Focus on the Family

Tools
- XO Marriage, marriage resource website by Jimmy Evans (https://xomarriage.com/)

## **Boundaries**

Havilah Cunnington
- I Do Boundaries

John Townsend & Henry Cloud
- Boundaries

Danny Silk
- Keep Your Love On

## Finances
Dave Ramsey
- The Total Money Makeover
- Dave Ramsey's Complete Guide to Money

Kris Vallotton
- Poverty, Riches and Wealth

## Other Topics
Jim Burns
- Doing Life with Your Adult Children

Stormie Omartian
- The Power of Praying for Your Adult Children

Dr. Caroline Leaf
- Cleaning Up Your Mental Mess

Jennie Allen
- Get Out of Your Head

Jenn Johnson
- All Things Lovely

The link to Patty Noel's testimony video:
https://fb.watch/aWvxR0KM6z/

Made in the USA
Coppell, TX
03 November 2022

85720854R00144